HOMESTEADING

HOMESTEADING

PERCY WOLLASTON

With a Foreword by Jonathan Raban

The Lyons Press

Design by Cindy LaBreacht

Printed in the United States of America

10 9 8 7 6 5 4 3 2 1

Wollaston, Percy, 1904–1983

    Homesteading / Percy Wollaston; with a foreword by Jonathan Raban.

        p.   cm.

    ISBN 1-55821-602-2

      1. Wollaston, Percy, 1904–1983—Childhood and youth.

    2. Pioneers —Montana—Ismay—Biography. 3. Frontier and pioneer life—Montana—Ismay. 4. Ismay (Mont.)—Biography.

    5. Ismay (Mont.)—Social life and customs. I. Title

    F739.I86W65   1997

    978.6'33—dc21

    [B]   97-16642

                                            CIP

CONTENTS

FOREWORD

In America time has a habit of moving faster than it does elsewhere: during the life of a single man or woman, the present slides into the historic past and history itself frays into mere romantic legend. The American way of building—tearing down the old and replacing it with the new—alters the landscape beyond recognition, robbing it of all the signs and clues that can make the recent past articulate and vivid. It is no wonder that American grandparents are chronic memoirists, for their own childhoods are likely to seem to their grandchildren as remote as the era of the Boston Tea Party or the Alamo.

So it was for Percy Wollaston when, sometime in 1972, he sat down at his elderly manual Smith-Corona and began to type this memoir, intended for his grandchildren. Myrtle, his wife, had died in May, and Percy, finding himself suddenly alone, returned to the land of his and Myrtle's childhood, recreating on the page the bare, dry country of eastern Montana in the teens of the century, its wide-open miles of sagebrush, shale, and buffalo grass. Writing in the age of Watergate and the aftermath of the Vietnam war, he transported himself back into that long-lost America of the Progressive Era, when faith in the idea of America, in American science, and technology, and education, had been at its dizzy zenith.

The contrast between the time in which he was writing and the time of which he wrote could hardly have been sharper. As he pecked out his descriptions of the arid, treeless landscape of his boyhood, he could look out the window to a dripping pine forest, and listen to the chuckle of a pellucid trout stream just a few yards from his door. As dryness had shaped his early years, so Percy had spent his adult life in the constant, comforting presence of water. He'd worked for Montana Power, first on the hydroelectric dam across the Clark Fork River at Thompson Falls, Montana, then on the dam across the Missouri River at Great Falls. When he retired, he and Myrtle settled in a handsome log-house in a clearing in the woods, near Eureka, Montana, on the wet, western slopes of the Rocky Mountains. Elk trespassed on his garden from the surrounding Kootenai National Forest. Grave Creek—ice-cold, boulder-strewn, dimpled with rising fish—ran past his lawn.

In *Where the Bluebird Sings to the Lemonade Springs*, Wallace Stegner wrote of how control of water is the key to the history of the West—a lesson instinctively absorbed by Percy Wollaston. He once told his youngest son, Michel, that his most abiding childhood memory was of seeing his mother on her knees, day after day, weeping, and praying for rain. When Percy fled the dry prairie after graduating from high school, he made a beeline for the water. Water meant security, income, insurance against heartbreak.

Before he wrote his book, he almost never spoke of the homestead on which he had grown up. He was a taciturn man, not given to flights of reminiscence, and Michel Wollaston came to understand that the family homestead near Ismay was a touchy subject with his father. Questioned about his childhood, Percy was habitually gruff. Then, in 1974, the father handed the son a sheaf of manuscript, saying it was nothing much, probably not worth the trouble of reading. After fifty years of bottling up the past, Percy had at last allowed it to come flooding back to him in memory—the story of that doomed community on the Montana prairie in which his parents had invested their lives, of an American dream that turned, literally, to dust.

The Wollastons were among the many thousands of people who were lured west by the passing of the Enlarged Homestead Act of 1909 and the extravagant promotional literature of the railroads. The government promised 320 acres of "semi-arid" land to anyone willing to cultivate it and erect a dwelling on it; the railroads (needing population to support their own westward march to the Pacific) set out to depict the land as boundlessly fertile, waiting only on the efforts of hardworking men and women to transform it into a green quilt of farms and busy market towns.

This was the heyday of unregulated advertising, when copy-writers were free to talk-up their products in the language of magic and miracles. The land was talked-up, relentlessly. The Chicago, Milwaukee, St. Paul & Pacific Railroad (this mouthful was usually condensed to "The Milwaukee Road"), which brought the Wollastons and their goods out to Montana, employed a band of prose-poets and fanciful artists to represent the prairie as a new Arcadia. The jacket-illustration to the company's most famous pamphlet showed a strangely clerk-like plowman, steering a single-bladed plow, drawn by two horses, across a map of the Montana section of the Milwaukee Road line. As the soil peeled away from the blade, it turned into a stream of gold coins, each one stamped with the figure of Liberty.

The pale shirt-sleeved plowman (evidently still unused to the outdoor life) was meant to signal that no farming experience was needed to cash in on this astonishing free offer. The text of the pamphlet recommended that the novice study the "Campbell Method" of "dry-farming" in order to ensure his or her success. The results that the novice might reasonably expect were attested to in photographs of spring wheat standing as thick as the bristles on a brush, of heaps of succulent fruits and vegetables, of acres of plowed, dark, level soil. Most of the photography, it seems, had been done on irrigated land close to the Yellowstone River—land that had long been taken up, and which bore precious little resemblance to the dry prairie, just a few miles away, that was actually available for homesteading.

The railroad brochures hymned the climate of eastern Montana: it was temperate, invigorating, medicinal—which would have come as news to anyone familiar with its regular summer droughts, its 40-below winters, its hail, its lightning storms, its plagues of grasshoppers. They made light of its scant rainfall, and bamboozled the reader with long-outdated pseudo-science. Rain follows the plow, claimed the copywriters; it follows settlement, it follows the railroads. Much was made of the Agassiz theory, 40 years old and conclusively disproved, that locomotives, passing at speed through a landscape, create some kind of electro-magnetic brouhaha, in which rain-clouds materialize out of nowhere, to water the crops sown close to the line. The homesteading region had been part of what was shown on old maps as The Great American Desert, but twentieth century science had solved the rainfall problem, and the would-be settler should have no fears on that score. On the green cloth front of Campbell's *Soil Culture Manual* was embossed, in gold, a camel, with a banner trailed across its legs. The banner read: "The Camel For The Sahara Desert, The Campbell Method For The American Desert." Campbell's method was a peculiar blend of Calvinist theology and kitchen-table science, in which capillary attraction was presented as a mystical nostrum, to be exploited by the "dry farmer." The method was largely hokum—and it was responsible for the destruction of much of the valuable topsoil in eastern Montana and the western Dakotas. But Campbell's *Manual* became the agricultural bible of the inexperienced homesteaders. In the first issue of Ismay's newspaper, *The Ismay*, in May 1908, there appeared a poem which nicely captures the spirit of the dry-farming craze, in which H.W. Campbell was the self-proclaimed evangelist:

HOMESTEADING

THE DRY LAND HOMESTEADER

I've started to dry-farm
A piece of bench land sod,
And if I meet no harm
I'll win or bust—by jinks.

Plow and harrow and disc—
Disc and harrow and plow:
Of course there is some risk
Until a chap knows how.

Campbell says they will grow
If seeds are put in right—
Depends on how you sow
With ground in proper plight.

And so I work all day:
At night I read his book—
I get no time to play
And hardly time to cook.

The pamphlets—addressed as much to the store clerk, the schoolteacher, the barber, the discharged soldier, as to the farmer—were printed in bulk and distributed through the overcrowded cities of the eastern United States. They found their way to Europe—to Bessarabia, Germany, Sweden, Norway, Ireland, England. They promised a new life in a green land to anyone who could muster the fare to Montana. Families spent their life-savings on the transatlantic passage, in steerage, to New York, and thence by rail on the long journey to the Far West. When they disembarked from the train, at Ismay, Mildred, or Terry, most were confounded by what they saw. The gently rolling farmland of the pamphlets turned out to be mile after mile of open range—bone-dry, dotted with the mushroom-shaped rock-formations of the badlands, without a sheltering tree in sight.

The Wollastons were not confounded. Unlike so many of their neighbors, they were used to the harsh climate and topography of the dry West, and they had every skill necessary for homesteading. If anyone could make this great experiment succeed, Ned Wollaston was qualified to do so.

Born in England, Ned was aged four when his father, a Liverpool shipping agent, also named Percy, took his family out to Fairfield, Minnesota in 1876. Percy Wollaston the elder was an unusually well-heeled immigrant. The descendant of a long line of intellectually-minded Anglican clergymen, Percy had done well in the shipping business. At 51, full of energy and hankering for a change of scene, he set out to make a splash in America. In the brand-new agricultural town of Fairfield, he helped found the Episcopalian church, became a banker, a farmer, a miller (his Norfolk-style windmill, with its 30-foot sails, became a famous landmark in the district), and the owner of the general store. To house his family, he built a 16-room mansion with landscaped grounds. Measured by the ordinary standards of the rural Midwest, the house was a palace: but Percy, whose energy wasn't confined to his commercial activities, had fathered thirteen children, of whom Ned was the youngest.

Ned grew up around the farm (his father was raising wheat and barley on a 460-acre spread of moist Minnesota soil). When he left home, he worked as a general hand on a cattle ranch near Dickinson, North Dakota, and became an expert horseman and carpenter. In 1900, aged 28, he returned briefly to Fairfield, where he married Dora Marietta, a young widow with a son named Raymond. Ned, Dora, and Ray then went west again—to Madison, South Dakota, where they ran a country store and farmed a small acreage two miles south of town. Here the younger Percy Wollaston was born in 1904.

In South Dakota, the Wollastons barely made ends meet. The passage through Congress of the Enlarged Homestead Act must have seemed a godsend to them. It promised a great increase of land, for free, less than four hundred miles west of where they were living. Yet this very closeness of eastern Montana to western North Dakota was, perhaps, a fatal delusion.

The true West—the dry West—is usually said to begin at around 100° W, which is the line of longitude that corresponds with an average annual rainfall of 15 inches. East of the line, there's more than 15", west, there's less. Madison, N.D., is 97°W—securely inboard of the dry/moist line. Ismay, MT., is a few miles short of 105°W, and rainfall there drops to an annual average of 11 or 12 inches; a modest difference, but a crucial one.

Experienced as Ned was, he too fell for the new scientific miracle of "dry farming." Conserve moisture. Loosen the top-soil. Pack the subsoil. Create a "reservoir" beneath the surface of your land. . . . The Campbell Method, and its many local variations, were agricultural gospel in 1909, when Ned Wollaston prepared to move his family to the vaunted free land of Montana.

The young Percy was six-going-on-seven when Ned auctioned off his unwanted goods in Madison and the family shipped out on the Milwaukee Road for their new life. It is a perfect age for the accumulation of photographically-brilliant memories. At seventy, Percy Wollaston was able to recall on paper the family's first days on the homestead with a child's promiscuously attentive eye. Nothing, it seems, was lost on him. All his life, he had been a practical man—a fine carpenter, a devoted gardener, a crack shot with a rifle. He had always attended patiently to details. Alone in his log-house by the river, he now attended to the details of his childhood on the homestead with the same scrupulous care that he brought to his woodworking.

He was not a practised writer. His wife Myrtle (who had grown up on a Norwegian-American homestead on Cabin Creek, a few miles east of Ismay, her childhood matching Percy's point for point) had been the literary member of the family; she and her sisters, known far and wide as "the Amundson girls," had opened a school on the prairie, and, as a mother, she had introduced her children to an impressively broad range of poetry and fiction. When Percy sat down to write a book, he may, perhaps, have been taking on the task that Myrtle had been promising to do before she died. Certainly his writing came as a great surprise to his children.

The wonder of it is that it is pitch-perfect. Unforced, unsentimental, often dryly funny, it has the ring of experience itself insisting on making itself manifest in writing. It tells the story of what now must seem a tragic episode in American history, but it tells it with artful reticence, withholding the tragedy, yet letting it impinge, by suggestion, on the narrative.

It is a three-dimensional portrait of the community of homesteaders which assembled on the prairie after the arrival of the Milwaukee Road. In the spirit of the settlers themselves, the book focuses on the high hopes, and the considerable achievements, of the homesteaders as they established their farms on the unforgiving land. Though Percy Wollaston alludes importantly to *Giants in the Earth*, the tone of *Homesteading* is a world away from that of Rollvag's grim epic. The casual reader, flipping through these pages, might mistake it for mere sunny-side-up cheerfulness.

But Wollaston was an instinctive ironist. If the main thrust of his story is about the brave resourcefulness of that makeshift society on the Montana prairie, its margins are darkly shadowed: disappointment, loneliness, sudden death, foolish incompetence are continually in evidence, and the book comes to be haunted by a horribly memorable suicide—all the more effectively rendered for being done in Percy Wollaston's habitual manner of laconic detachment. The reader grows to understand, by inference, that this is a story of a colossal failure.

From 1917 onwards, the homesteaders began to flee the land to which they had come with bold and optimistic dreams. They were exhausted and bankrupted by a combination of brutal cold, drought, falling wheat prices and a burden of debt, taken on when bank loans were cheap and easy (see Percy Wollaston on the smiling bank manager, Hayden Bright). Credit was as much to blame, in the end, as the Montana weather.

The Wollastons survived longer than most of their immediate neighbors. They bought a car (a Model T), but they did not go in for the expensive farm machinery—the tractors and threshers—that led so many to penury. Ned continued to plow with horses. Dora's trade in butter, eggs, and honey kept the household alive when cattle died and the wheat crop failed.

Percy left in 1924, taking the train west to the Pacific, and, it was vaguely said, "to college." He probably intended to try for a place at the University of Washington in Seattle, the western terminus of the Milwaukee Road. But when his train pulled in at Thompson Falls, a forest fire was raging along the mountainside, and all able-bodied men aboard the train were asked to volunteer to fight it. When the fire was under control, Percy stayed put. For the next year, he worked for the Forest Service as a "smoke-chaser," living a Huckleberry Finn existence in the woods above Thompson Falls. Then, with his impending marriage to Myrtle much in mind, he took a job with Montana Power on the hydroelectric dam: to a young man who had grown up amid so much failure, so many blighted hopes, the value of company housing, health-care, and a pension scheme was already apparent. Homesteading was the epitome of the life of Emersonian self-reliance and proud financial independence. Percy's experience of that life evidently led him to settle gratefully for a niche in corporate—and watery—America.

His parents followed him to Thompson Falls in 1926. Ned and Dora were drained, but not penniless. Most of the homesteads in the neighborhood were simply abandoned, to be reclaimed by the county for their unpaid taxes. Ned retained his title to the Wollaston place, and even found a tenant to pay him a peppercorn rent on it. Arrived in Thompson Falls, he was able to muster $550 to buy about two-thirds of an acre of land overlooking the river, where he built a house that was a small replica of the homestead on the prairie. The Wollastons had escaped lightly. Their small utopian democracy, centered around the Whitney Creek schoolhouse, had collapsed about their ears, but they were among the least seriously injured victims of the catastrophe.

I n 1994, Michel Wollaston and I drove to Montana, to look for whatever might remain of the homestead. The land had reverted, long ago, to open range. The prairie was dotted with wrecked houses, most of them vacated relatively recently, in the 1950s and 60s, and rusted farm machinery. Of the homestead society described by Percy Wollaston, little was left except for a few weathered fenceposts trailing whiskers of barbed wire. The schoolhouse described in the book was still, just, in business; it had two students, and was due to close forever in the summer of '94. The meadowlarks and killdeer plovers appeared to now have most of eastern Montana to themselves: I had never seen a lonelier landscape, where the dead so outnumbered the living, and where the wreckage of failed enterprises was the most conspicuous human feature of the place.

We found the "swale" of the brook—a zig-zag seasonal creek, running west-to-east, with a long low bluff on its southern bank. A lone cottonwood tree marked the site of

Ned's spring. It took us a while to figure where the house must have been. We carried Percy's sketch of the homestead and its outbuildings, and tried holding it up at various points along the swale until at last the picture and the land made a perfect fit.

Then, quite suddenly, we couldn't walk a step without stumbling on a further relic of the family past. Here, buried in the dirt, were the flaky remains of a milk churn; there, a piece of a wooden wagon-wheel. We found a child's broken sled (Percy's?), identifiable bits of a Model T, the front of a cooking stove, half a toy pistol. We parted the grass to uncover the foundations of the house that Ned had built; the flagstone path from the kitchen to the hen-house was still intact.

As a 12- and 13-year-old, I had spent summers helping to dig up the remains of Roman villas in Winchester. Archeologising on the prairie, brushing dirt off rusty artifacts, made the Wollastons' twentieth century past seem almost as remote and forlorn as the buried civilization of those ancient conquerors, with their centrally-heated terra-cotta floors, their fine Samian ware (the glaze on the shards of pottery still vivid in 1954), their silver *denarii* (so easily mistakable for the English sixpenny piece). The homesteaders, like the Romans, had believed that they'd be here for ever—building stout houses for their succeeding generations. Eighty years on, their prairie empire had gone the way of Roman Britain.

On the north side of the swale, between the house and the spring, we found a spot where the buffalo grass grew thinly over an irregular patch of black dirt. There'd been a bonfire here. Digging with my fingernails, I unearthed a small silver medallion. The head of a Greek goddess was stamped on it. A broken hinge—or something—was attached to its edge.

I handed it to Mike, who put on his reading glasses and studied it in his open palm.

"I think I know what this is. It's the clasp from an old-timey photograph album." He handed it back to me. "They must have burned the family photos when they left."

If they had burned the family photos, it was easy to imagine why. Leaving the homestead, Ned and Dora could not bear to take with them the record of their own guileless optimism—the smiling faces, the half-built barns, the new plow, the new horse . . . the new life in all its pristine possibility.

That would explain Percy Wollaston's lifelong taciturnity when it came to speaking of the homestead. But as the years passed, the absence of that record must have made itself felt as a sad loss that had to be repaired. In place of the burned album, we have a book; and it is infinitely more vivid than the faded Brownie snapshots could possibly have been.

—Jonathan Raban

PUBLISHER'S NOTE

The manuscript of *Homesteading* is a continuous narrative, without headings or breaks of any kind. The publisher has inserted the chapter titles simply as hand-holds for the reader; but they are the publisher's words, not Wollaston's. On a few occasions, when Wollaston had abandoned a train of thought and later returned to it, an editorial decision has been made to move a few paragraphs of text, so that the story flows more naturally. The occasional misspelling and such has been corrected, but otherwise *Homesteading* appears as Percy Wollaston wrote it.

PIONEERS

To most of us, the term "pioneer" brings forth a vision of some buckskin-clad individual, hardy and tough, out of the far-distant past, but in reality we are all of us pioneers in our time, wearing the clothes that are most suitable or available, making the best of the present situation and learning to cope with new conditions.

So it was with the people who homesteaded Eastern Montana. Hardy they were, indeed. They had to be. If some of them were tough it was from sheer necessity and not a matter of choice. The rare individual who thought he would like to be tough all too soon got the opportunity and flunked the test. Clothing finally settled down to big overalls and shirt for men and gingham dresses for women, but at first there was a hodgepodge of whatever the people had brought with them. Shoes were whatever the individual had or could afford and hats, for a longer time than anything else, remained what its wearer had been accustomed to in the former home.

The trapper, the hunter, the gold-seeker, the cattleman and the sheepman had all come in rapid succession and there were still a few who had seen and survived all these changes. It was from these early-timers that the settler got his best advice and began to adapt himself to the land.

The land itself was inexorable: The bed of some prehistoric ocean, it had tolerated only the creatures that were best able to survive, resisting even the elements by presenting an ever-harder surface or a more soil-clutching grass to the ravages of erosion.

I

HOMESTEADING

The Northern Pacific railroad had been built through the central part of the state, following the Yellowstone River and people were beginning to spread out from its little towns but the livestock interests dominated the scene and the settler was more or less ignored. All the correspondence and reports of the earliest comers had brought on a growing interest and awareness of the new territory so by the time the Milwaukee Road approached the area, a flood of people were in the mood to try their luck in a new land.

I believe the Milwaukee Road construction stopped for the winter of 1907-08 at Mowbridge, South Dakota where the line crosses the Missouri River. The bridge was completed and work stopped somewhere near there for the winter. Here was a new route to a new land and any number of people, land-hungry and looking for a place to settle. That they would be settling on land already in use for grazing by established ranches was a matter that few considered. Fewer yet had any idea of the requirements of the land.

As the railroad advanced in the spring of 1908, so did the wave of new people. Each little way-station had its store, hotel of sorts, post office, saloon and maybe even a barbershop. Someone set up as a "locator" to help other newcomers to find land and locate their section corners. I don't know whether there was such a thing as a chamber of commerce in those days, but nobody saw any reason why his town shouldn't grow to a thriving metropolis and promptly set about seeing that it did by encouraging others to settle in that area.

Homesteading, to me, was an adventure only, with none of the cares or hardships experienced by my elders, and my account can be only the recollections of a child or boy, hazy and distorted by time, inaccurate at best: a poor memoir for the hundreds of people who struggled so hard to make their homes.

One should be able to begin a story with the conventional "Once upon a time" and have done with it, but what time? Any one of the factors influencing the advance of settlement would be a story in itself and each settler had some different reason for the move.

My first inkling of a change came somewhere between 1908 and 1910 when we came to Montana. I remember my parents discussing something about "taking up a claim." The imagination and curiosity of a four or five year old boy began to conjure up pictures of some vague object being taken up bodily. This must have been about the same time that the Indians of Dakota were dealt out of some of their Standing Rock Reservation for homestead purposes as I remember Dad saying he "Wouldn't mind taking a shot at Standing Rock" and pictured him shooting at a large stone column. On another evening Mother said "Percy and I could hold down the claim if you had to go somewhere to find work" and I envisioned Mother and myself trying to hold down a huge tarp or canvas in a terrific wind

Dad and Mother were renting a farm at Madison, South Dakota and early in the spring of 1910 Dad went to Montana to locate the new home. At that time one could file for a homestead of 320 acres, or a half section of land.

We chose a location that had a good spring, its permanence indicated by old buffalo and stock trails converging. There was some land suitable for farming, some for pasture and was near an area which he thought no sensible person would homestead but which would be good summer range for stock: His plan was to farm what was necessary for feed while building up a small ranch. The idea of any open range was soon to fail because all available land, however worthless as a homestead, was taken up as claims.

To the Southwest about ten miles there was a belt of pine timber which could furnish logs and firewood. Later a small community sawmill was set up there and lumber sawed for building construction. About five miles to the East there was a vein of lignite coal and slightly farther was a belt of juniper which was to furnish posts for the whole area.

About the first of September, an auction was held to dispose of items that would not be needed or could not be taken. The average settler could only afford the freight costs of one immigrant car and all stock or equipment must be shipped in it.

Now that we were really committed to the move, we were regaled with stories of fantastic migrations of rattlesnakes to or from their denning places or tales of blizzard and storm where the hero was never found.

Dad had spent ten years as a cowpuncher and horserancher near Dickinson, North Dakota, so he had a fairly good idea of the conditions to be met and what equipment would be needed, but I think the wild tales and misinformation influenced a lot of the newcomers into bringing some odd and ill chosen equipment.

The freight car was loaded with the stock in one end, household goods in the other and a small living space left in the middle. Four horses, two cows, a dismantled wagon and bobsled and some baled hay filled one end of the car. As I remember, there was no regular loading platform available and some sort of ramp was used. The horses were led on docilely enough but the cows were a different matter and a good deal of pulling and tail-twisting ensued before they were tied in their makeshift stall. Some chickens, a dog and two cats in a cage comprised the rest of the livestock.

Dad and my oldest brother, Harold, were to go in the immigrant car, my older brother, Raymond, was to spend the winter with an uncle in Minnesota in order to attend school and Mother and I were to follow a few days later by train when the initial camp was established.

For some reason, I remember the date, September twenty-second, when we arrived in Mildred, Montana. The town consisted of a store, saloon and hotel all one large building, the depot, coal docks stockyard, and a few other buildings. The store was operated by M.M. and L.H. Clark who were to prove mainstays of the community almost as long as the town was active.

The day was chilly, a drizzling rain was falling and a general gloom seemed to have settled over the land. Ten miles by wagon in the rain seems like a long time to a child and I think we passed only one homestead on the way. This was the homestead of Mr. and Mrs. Murphy who must have settled in 1908 as their place was fenced and they had a tall two story house. I can still see the road as it appeared then as at that time the only road went through their place and past their front door. The gateway was marked by high cedar posts which were about fifteen feet tall. This was often done in order that the traveller could recognize the gate at a distance and to act as a landmark in storms. We were greeted by the Murphys in passing and, I think, given some cantaloupes or vegetables.

It was evening when we reached our new home, a tent with a canvas-covered pile of household furniture in front of it. I believe even the cookstove was outside and cooking was done on a campfire. Whatever the arrangements, it was Home, our family was together, a few familiar pieces of furniture were there to be seen even if there wasn't room to use them.

The cats, after the manner of their kind, had taken up their residence among the furniture under the canvas cover. Here was something familiar to use as a base of exploration in a strange land, protection from the rain or imagined enemies and near to their family. We were soon to appreciate their value, for the mice began seeking shelter from the rain or homes for the coming winter. Grain for the horses was also stored under the canvas and there would soon have been little left for the horses without an efficient guard.

I might as well mention the rodent population here as all settlers promptly discovered that quite large quantities of grain could vanish overnight, silverware and trinkets disappeared or were transferred to weird hiding places and stored clothes were used as nesting places. The native grasses furnished excellent cover and food for hordes of mice. There was one little fellow with the instincts of a packrat: Not many of them but one or two would in a night transfer several quarts of grain from its place to an empty boot or a bureau drawer. I suspect that they have gone the way of the prairie dog and the wild ferret. Every sheltering ledge of rocks had its family of packrats or a cottontail rabbit. The patches of buckbrush furnished homes for colonies of the shorttailed meadow or field mice. This was a land of abundance for the small creatures: The coyote, weasel, hawk, owl and ferret maintained a balance.

Few families had had the good sense or foresight to think of bringing old Tabby but now the owner of a family of cats was almost as welcome as Dick Whittington and kittens were spoken for months ahead. Most of the established ranches had one or two sedate and venerable tomcats who had survived years of raids by coyote and owl but ranchers knew the value of their pets and treated them as members of the household.

Chill, rainy weather continued for several days but the dog, Pat, and I amused ourselves exploring the new land. I gathered cow chips for fuel but the dampness had made them temporarily useless. There were still a few piles of buffalo bones to be found and on the nearest knoll or rise of ground where the hunters had concealed themselves I would gather the spent cartridges. Generally they were fairly long cases of forty calibre or larger: One that I remember was 40-82 and I think a 50-90 but cannot recall that for sure. I got a piece of glass and spent much time scraping buffalo horns to polish them but that soon palled as amusement.

The work of hauling lumber from town went on regardless of weather as a house and shelter for the stock had to be put up before winter, hay must be located for the stock and no end of other chores all needing to be done immediately.

Finally the skies cleared, the weather became balmy and we had Indian Summer at its best. Montana smiled its most enticing smile, seeming to assure the unwary that there was no such thing as bad weather. We noticed that the cows would graze for only a short time and then lie down contentedly. They had grazed almost continually in Dakota and at first we thought there was something wrong with them but then realized that there was more nutrition in the grass so that they were quickly satisfied.

BUILDING OUR HOUSE

One fine afternoon work stopped and Dad and Mother set out to decide for the permanent building site. They chose a site with a nice view about a quarter of a mile from the spring but if they had realized the difficulty of striking good water or any water at all I believe they would have built close to where the water was already available. The absence of water was to be an enduring problem to most of the settlers and many a thirty or forty foot "duster" was dug by hand.

The house-building progressed rapidly as there again Dad's experience paid off; he had worked as a carpenter at various times and seemed to be capable of building or repairing almost anything. The house was two-story with a single large room downstairs and another upstairs, which was divided by curtains and the placing of a large dresser in the middle. As soon as possible we moved into the house and construction of a barn was begun: The house was far from complete but there was always the possibility of bad weather and shelter for the stock must be made before then. The barn was made as a half dugout; that is, a place was dug back into a hill until the bank thus formed could be used as the back wall. Tall posts were set up for the front and shorter ones for the sides as the slope of the hill required. A framework of poles was built on these posts and a layer of poles laid closely together on the top. A thick layer of hay was laid on the roof poles, a layer of dirt then shovelled over the hay and then the front was closed in with lumber. Digging an excavation large enough for a building, even a small one is not a chore to be done with pick and shovel unless one has time and energy to spare. Here again foresight and preparation had paid off as there was a slip scraper brought along with that first carload of goods. A man with a team and scraper can move a lot of dirt in a day.

What is a slip scraper? I'd forgotten that you might not know. They were a large iron scoop with handles so that the operator could tilt it in order to dig into the ground. When full, it was simply allowed to drag until time to empty it, when the handles were raised high enough for the scraper to begin digging. A little more raising caused it to flip over and empty.

There were posts to be cut and hauled from "The Cedars," that belt of juniper some five miles to the East. There were poles to be cut and hauled from "The Pines" ten or more miles to the Southwest and the hay for the roof came from the Alex McDonald ranch about six miles to the Northwest. Each of these trips meant a long day of hard work, and, more especially, a day of precious time.

I often think what a difficult time this must have been for Harold. A large, slow-moving boy, inclined to fat, he had not yet passed the clumsy age or attained full growth but was still expected to perform a man's work with a grown man's skill. Later to be immensely strong and astonishingly quick, he was now clumsy and his budding strength only brought upon him the heavier tasks.

HOMESTEADING

As soon as the barn was built for the horses an addition was started for the cows. Posts were set up for the corners and doorway and the roof frame made. Some of the wall was made by nailing woven wire fencing on each side of the upright posts and packing hay or straw between them but there was a little less hurry about this as the first barn would serve for emergency shelter. Now a lean-to kitchen was added to the West side of the house and a rough storage and coalshed on the north, gravel being spread in the angle thus formed to serve as a walkway until some time when flagstones could be laid.

There were occasional light snows and freezing nights by now but most of the weather was mild, with clear sunny days and quite warm afternoons. I used to see pieces of gypsum or mica glinting on the hillsides but was some time finding it because the angle of the light changed as I approached. We saw long flights of sandhill cranes going south and then finally long vees of geese. On the day that the roof of the cowbarn was finished, we got the first real storm. How thankful we all felt to have been granted time to provide comfortable shelter! We could gather around a warm stove in the evenings. The water bucket might be frozen in the morning but we had no thought of this being any great hardship.

One morning I looked in the barn door and, wonder of wonders, there was a new calf! Trembling, wet and steaming, it had not even gotten to its feet yet and its mother was giving it a bath. I had seen older calves many times before and taken them for granted but here was something different entirely and after the first awestruck gaze I bolted to spread the news. I learned long later that this event had been planned and timed for late Fall in order to furnish a supply of fresh milk and butter during the winter.

OUR FIRST THANKSGIVING

In common with most growing boys, my memory was connected directly to my stomach: The clearest recollections center around that old lean-to kitchen. The crackle of juniper kindling, the rasp of coffee being ground in the mill, the clink of stove lids, the thump of the reservoir cover when warm water was taken out for washing, and the sizzle of frying bacon. The bacon is something no one is going to believe nowadays. There was only enough fat left after frying it to furnish grease for the pancake griddle. Hickory smoked, solid lean meat with only little streaks of fat interlarding it. Only once, since, in some country-cured bacon have I seen anything even approaching it. What we get as bacon now resembles what was called sowbelly then. That came in wide strips, was heavily salted, smoked very little, if any, and was nearly all fat, as is our bacon nowadays. This was used as 'fried salt pork' or to mix with baked beans, boiled cabbage, etc. Lard was sold in five, ten and fifty pound tin containers; you didn't get it when you paid for bacon.

The five-pound lard pail and the two-pound tobacco box served as the standard lunch-pail for school, work lunches and such for several years. The ten-pound pail served as a small water-bucket, storage of beans or dried fruits and as a sort of standard in measure. The fifty-pounder came in a wooden crate which could serve as a stool, packing box or any number of uses. The can itself was prized as a storage container for flour, sugar and the like. I can still see 'Swift's Silver Leaf Lard' shining in its crate.

Mother used to often put a small sprig of juniper or the berries or a few leaves of the sagebrush on the hot stove. What fragrance! The woodbox was the favorite roosting place for boy and man alike. The warmth and security of a fire, the smell of good food and the presence of an understanding woman was a magnet to any male and the country woodbox was the seat of more plans, confidence and confessions than any other.

With the coming of Thanksgiving, we began to get acquainted with our nearest neighbors. These were the Docken brothers, Will and Art, who I think must have come in the Spring of 1910 or the year before and Frank and Leigh Roberts. I think the Roberts boys were cousins of the Dockens. Will Docken lived a mile and a half to the East and it was through his yard that Dad and Harold had been going to The Cedars and The Coal Mine. His brother Art had a log cabin on land adjoining his to the Southeast. The Roberts boys lived some two or three miles North of him. Through these connections Dad had become acquainted with them and they were invited to our house for Thanksgiving dinner.

Thanksgiving Day was beautifully clear, with about six inches of snow and just cold enough to make everything sparkle. I remember seeing the four of them come walking up the valley from Will Docken's place where they had gathered. Here were NEW NEIGHBORS whom Mother and I had never seen before. Bachelors all, the Docken boys were probably in their late thirties, the Roberts boys younger. Art Docken had been in the Spanish American War, Leigh Roberts had been in the navy in 1908 when President Teddy Roosevelt sent them around the world. So we began a series of friendships that were to last for years and stand the tests of a good many hardships.

I don't remember any details of the day or the dinner other than seeing these young men arrive in a group and learning some small detail of each one, yet that meeting somehow bound us together as a group or community from that day forward. Probably this same thing was happening all over the area, cementing little groups of individuals into working neighborhood units.

COAL AND CEDAR

The Coal Mine was situated at a place known to the ranchers and old time residents as Rock Springs due to some enormous sandstone formations there. It was in a deep sandy gully overlooked by the fortress-like rocks and pillars and there was a good spring of water there. Any permanent source of water was a landmark in that area and of course had been named long ago by the stockmen and travellers but to us it always remained The Coal Mine.

The coal was a low grade lignite vein about three feet thick. The sandy overburden was stripped off with the slip scraper which had been used in digging the place for the barn. I think the Docken brothers teamed up with Dad and Harold on this work and it was the beginning of work-sharing projects over the years. We began to hear rumors of accidents and cave-ins at other mining sites over the country where people had dug under the overburden without shoring or safe mining procedures. People who had never even handled a shovel before were now trying to scratch a winter's fuel from an unforgiving earth which tolerated few mistakes.

We used to find the formations of knots and leaves in the coal and one time turned up a live toad in a little pocket hollowed in the coal. The egg must have been washed into a crevice, hatched, and somehow survived, scratching out its little living space as it grew. It was without color and seemed to be blind. How it gained enough sustenance to live, I can't imagine.

Lignite coal has a large percentage of waste, clinkers and is inclined to slake down to a powder, so that it will smoulder in burning and produce quite large quantities of gas whenever there isn't sufficient draft to keep a good blaze going. This was the cause of a number of families being burned out of their homes in the dead of winter, and was always a hazard to be considered in leaving a stove unattended for even a short time: usually the gas formed in smouldering would finally ignite with only a slight whoof, blowing out a puff of sulphurous smoke and a handful of ashes into the room, but at times there was a 'whump' that banged the closed damper back on its hinges, threw live coals for several feet and was enough to startle the whole household, with drowsy cats and dogs leaping to their feet as though a shot had been fired.

Beyond the coal mine lay The Cedars, that belt of juniper I mentioned earlier. Here was the source of durable posts for the coming fencing projects, and I would wager that here and

COAL AND CEDAR

there, over the area, there are still vestiges of these first posts to be found in place. Some of the posts rotted fairly quickly, according to the type of ground or condition of the post but some of them seemed indestructible. Each settler chose a spot or pocket of timber as his, made some sort of access road to it and began cutting posts. There were large, gnarled trees, some of them probably two or three hundred years old. These were low shrubs, twisted and dwarfed by the elements but fairly large in diameter. The larger ones were split with wedges into post size. The beautiful reds and creamy whites of this wood deserved the treatment of skilled cabinet makers rather than to be used as posts.

There was something enchanting about these juniper pockets that I have found in no other place. There were scattered trees on the hills but the real thickets were in the heads of little canyons, surrounded by the steep gumbo cliffs and the weird rock formations of the area. Here was the aroma of juniper, the twittering of chickadees and a tranquility that had lasted for untold ages.

It seems ironic that the peaceful juniper pockets should be the scene of the first real quarrels among the settlers, but as the number of people increased so did the post-cutting areas decrease. Settlers not only wanted to cut posts for their own use but, since cash money was practically nonexistent, the posts became a fine medium of exchange. A few late comers, finding access already prepared to a good location, moved in and started cutting on an area that someone else had worked for days to build a trail to. There were some near fights and some threatening with axes but in the long run, the fellow in the wrong had the less determination and hunted a post supply of his own.

An area a mile long and half a mile wide takes a lot of posts to surround it. Add to this division fences to enclose fields or confine stock for pasture, fences around haystacks and gardens or farmyards and one begins to realize the work entailed in just enclosing one of these homesteads.

In our case, post cutting went on all winter whenever weather permitted. The men left almost as soon as daylight allowed and returned well after dark. We used to listen for the clink of trace chains and the crunch and squeal of the wagon tires in the snow. I don't think there is anything that can make cold seem more penetrating or dismal than that creak of wagon tires in cold snow.

Mother would place a lamp on the table so that it would shine through the window toward the road to the East and it could be seen for a mile. How long that last mile must have seemed to the tired man and boy on some of those cold evenings! Still loads to be unloaded, chores to be done and preparation for another day.

CHRISTMAS

I mentioned the Murphy family whom we met on the way to our new home. They were an elderly couple with a son, Lou, who I believe was away at the time, possibly attending college. Mr. Murphy had planted two or three acres of cantaloupe and had a fine crop except that there was practically no market and the cantaloupe did not ripen all at the same time. These were the first cantaloupe we had ever seen and they were delicious. Smaller than the ones we see now, usually, but especially firm and good. We had seen only the large smooth-skinned muskmelon before.

Mrs. Murphy, as a girl, had nearly died of tuberculosis, being so low as to be confined to her sickbed, but her determination carried her along: She insisted on being carried out to a chair on the porch and stayed there in almost any sort of weather. She finally gained strength to stand, then to take a step by herself and made up her mind to take one more step each day. She said it was a great triumph for her when she was able to walk all the way to their front gate. At the time we made their acquaintance she was as hale a looking person as one might wish to see, and lived for many years after that.

The Murphys farmed for several years, but after Mr. Murphy's death, Mrs. Murphy and son Lou moved to town, where he became interested in banking and real estate.

Tuberculosis was a common ailment in those days and it, or the threat of weak lungs and poor health, was the deciding factor in causing many settlers to come to the open country. I don't think the Murphys came for that reason, as she was in excellent health then but I cite them rather as an example of the type of courage and determination some of these people had.

Shortly before Christmas I was allowed to go on one of the post-cutting trips to The Cedars. While the men worked I wandered around looking for a Christmas tree, finally deciding upon a small pitchpipe sapling, the only one of its kind in sight. I can't remember ever seeing another pitch pine that would have made a very attractive Christmas tree but this one has always embodied all the magic of Christmas and to this day sometimes the smell of pine conjures up the image of that first little tree.

On Christmas eve we went to spend the evening with the Morrow family. Jim Morrow had married my sister, who was seventeen years older than I and they had lived in Minneapolis until 1908 when they moved to Montana. Their oldest son, Rowland, was only nine months younger than I. Due to the difference in age I had never got to really know my sister or her family but Jim had helped Dad locate his place and I suppose they were the main factor in our settling where we did. Their story would be a fascinating book if properly told and I'll come back to some small account of them later.

The Christmas gathering consisted of Jim and Lorna, their three small sons, Rowland, Russel and Luard, Jim's married brother Fred and his wife, Florence, and an unmarried brother and sister of Jim's, Billie and Marie. The house was similar to ours, with one large downstairs room and a large lean-to kitchen. The tree was juniper, reaching to the ceiling and decorated with strings of popcorn and with red tapers made by twisting tissue paper around a pencil. There were a few candles clipped to the outer tips of the branches. These were a few candles clipped to the outer tips of the branches. These were only lighted at the very climax of the affair and a guard stood by with a waterbucket in case of fire.

As the time drew near for Santa to arrive, there was a good deal of scurrying, and consultation in whispers out in the kitchen. In a house that small and with that many people there isn't much chance for secrecy but finally Santa arrived to a rattle of trace chains for sleigh bells and gay cheering by all. There was Florence, a large, jolly woman with a lame foot and an unmistakable laugh in fourbuckle overshoes, a long, black, man's coat, disguised by a halloween mask of a leering, red nosed character with a huge bruise on one cheek; all this topped with a scotch cap. Rowland and I and possibly Russel were old enough to know very well who was behind the mask, but the spirit of Christmas was there and Santa, for the few brief minutes that the candles were lit, embodied all the magic and legend of Christmas.

After the ceremony and a few carols, we drove home nine miles of chill winter night, with a heated rock wrapped in sacks to keep our feet from freezing. I could blissfully snuggle under the laprobes and dream of the miracle but for my parents it must have been a different matter.

I have no recollection of Christmas day. Whether we had company or not or what we did, I can't remember. The main event was over and any further festivities or presents must not have made much impression on me.

SPRING'S WORK

Spring finally came, with its first meadowlarks and its crocus blooms, its sound of the running creek. The ground became soft enough for postholes to be dug and the fencing started. Then the day when the plow was gotten out and Dad started the first furrow. That was a ceremony in itself, to see the first of the long strips of sod turn like a wave away from the blade of the plow.

Much of the grass was what we called niggerwool and I don't know any other name for it. It was a very short, curly grass, highly nutritious and nature's own answer to soil conservation. The roots matted together so that the sod would turn in strips several feet long before breaking. Just under the grass there was a black layer of fine rich soil from half to three quarters of an inch thick. I realize now that this was the accumulation of centuries of fertilization and the only really good soil there was.

As the furrows turned, fat, white grubworms were exposed, each from a little round cubicle, and the blackbirds soon learned to follow the plow to pick them up. The mice and the gophers were turned out of their burrows and sought shelter under the sods that had been turned. No one knew or thought of contour farming then and the straight, unerring furrow, up hill and down dale, was the hallmark of a good plowman. Here there were plenty of hills and dales and the land, so outraged, soon began to take its toll.

I don't know how many acres of ground were broken or planted that Spring. Not very much, I'm sure, for in the Fall, Dad took the entire crop to market in one load. Not a very large load at that, and I sensed the frustration and worry as he and Mother looked at that small result of all their work.

That same Spring we acquired a new neighbor on the north half of our section. A middle-aged, garrulous Irish bachelor by the name of John Conlon: Addicted to Corn Cake tobacco, (which came in large, quart size sacks and smelled horribly), he firmly believed in the existence of hoop snakes, milk snakes, and ghosts and he once saw a large anaconda-type snake in one of the deep pools of Whitney Creek. Milk snakes sucked the milk cows and hoop snakes were a real menace. They would form a hoop by putting their tails in their mouth and roll downhill toward their intended victim. The tail terminated in a highly venomous horny spike and by lashing out with its tail as it terminated its roll downhill, the snake was sure death to whatever it struck; even oak trees, struck by this terrible viper, would soon wither and die. He was a fine, helpful and friendly neighbor who loved to visit, was always welcome, was afraid of dogs, who took advantage of him by loud barking, and he had absolutely no sense of direction after dark. He would stay visiting at our place or at the Docken's until some ten o'clock which was late in those times and then set off afoot for home. We all left our light burning for him until he had had time to round the hill that hid his place from ours in order for him to keep his bearings. Once or twice he spent most of the night wandering around trying to find home. More of his confusion later, but he endeared himself to our community and became known to us all as Uncle Johnny.

NEIGHBORS

The Striker family moved in on the homestead cornering ours to the Southwest. There were thirteen children, the youngest a girl of about twelve, so they really made an addition to the community. The mother had been crippled with

HOMESTEADING

inflammatory rheumatism from the time shortly after the youngest child was born and was confined to a wheel chair, only able to move her hands slightly. Mr. Striker was a large, heavily bearded man, very slow and precise in speech and very courteous. All the children were large; big, strapping men and women, slow moving, confident, friendly, and all keeping Maw as the center their activities. Whatever was planted in the garden or whatever was built was described to Maw in detail; its place and its progress. It always amazed me to see one of those towering men come into the house and say, "Maw, where's the wire stretcher?" or, "Maw, where's the hammer?" Maw would be able to tell them because she had the up-to-the-minute news of what each member of the family was doing. We liked and admired them all and they played a large part in the development of our community.

The Zehm family moved in two miles to the North with, I believe, six children, two of them grown men. We saw very little of them for the first year as they were out of our line of travel and everyone was too busy to do much social visiting. I don't know how they got moved or settled on their place, as at first they had no horse and Mr. Zehm used to walk the six miles to the cedars and carry wood home on his back. He was later to return from some such trip late in the afternoon and dine on some left-over chicken from the family's noon meal, dying that night of food poisoning. He is buried there on their homestead and the only flowers any of us were able to produce for the funeral was a small cardboard cross covered with the few geranium blossoms from Mother's one or two potted plants.

BUILDING THE SCHOOL

A Mr. Worsell and his son Arthur, about nine at that time moved onto a claim about a mile to the Southeast of us. Mr. Worsell had grown up in London, been a member of the Guards, later a lumberjack in the Minnesota woods and lost his wife when Arthur was three.

About three miles to the Southeast were the Young, Gilbert, and Faust families. All these three wives were fine-looking Norwegian sisters; they lived on adjoining homesteads and so formed a little unit of the community by themselves.

BUILDING THE SCHOOL

All the new arrivals called for a school and in the early fall or late summer of 1911 the heads of these households got together to form a school district and build a school. There was the Jarrett family of several children, also the McAtee family with, I think, three children. These families were about six miles to the south of us.

A more or less central location for the school was chosen out of this group of surrounding homesteads and I believe Mr. McAtee contributed the Northwest corner of his claim for the school ground, probably an acre in area. As I recall now, Mr. Striker, Mr. Jarrett, and, I think, a Mr. Harnack, a neighbor of the Youngs were chosen as school board members.

The school was built according to the specifications of that time, I'm sure, because there was some discussion as to the window area. The building dimensions, as planned, came out about half a window area short of that required by law, so another window was put in. This seems a small matter now but was an important financial decision at that time.

We now had a school and no teacher. A Professor Todd with wife and son had moved in recently as neighbors to the Youngs but he was too busy establishing a home to consider teaching just then, but would be willing to teach later. There was the Smith family, with three boys. One of them, Earl, had finished grade school and possibly had attended some high school. The other two were ready for the seventh and eighth grade. Earl Smith became our first teacher and taught until some time in the spring when he left to put in his crop.

I have never, anywhere or at any time, seen better discipline in a schoolroom or a teacher who gave more to the student. Any whispering or inattention brought a snap of his fingers which restored instant attention to the business of learning. When recess came, he was one of the kids, joining in the fun and tactfully seeing that there were no arguments. The world lost a natural and gifted educator when Earl went back to his farm.

I had started some schooling at home during the previous winter and now the whole panorama of eight grades was laid before us in one small schoolroom. The cadence of Evangeline and Snowbound soon held more appeal than "see baby run" and we were eager to reach those goals. The one room school may have a lot of drawbacks but it seems to me that it is an asset for the lower grades to be prepared for the upper ones.

It was now my brother Harold's turn to attend school and he was sent to stay with the uncle in Minnesota while Raymond was to go to the new school just formed. His schooling was destined to be cut short that winter as Mother had to return to Madison, South Dakota for an operation for cancer of the breast. Raymond was left to care for the stock, keep house, make and sell butter and do all that both my parents had been doing.

DYNAMITE

By the fall of 1911 we had a well. Dug by hand, using dynamite to break the worst layers of rock and hoisting the dirt to the surface by windlass it had been sunk to a depth of about thirty feet, producing a trickle of extremely hard, alkaline water sufficient for drinking purposes and household cooking only. Until you developed an immunity to its affects, it was almost the equivalent of Epsom salts.

Dynamite was about as easy to acquire as plug tobacco. If you bought it, you were assumed to know how to use it. The detonators were the dangerous element and because of their innocent appearance, they sometimes caused accidents. A blacksmith laid one on his anvil and hit it with a sledge; he wasn't harmed because the angle of his hammer deflected the blast, but the sledge went through the roof. A man in Terry, a town about thirty miles from us, was doing some digging on the outskirts of town. When he came to rock he got five sticks of dynamite for the job. Now, somehow, a general belief had grown up that the main force of the blast went down, even if the explosive was not confined in any way. He simply laid the five sticks on top of the rock and set off the charge. Five sticks of unconfined dynamite can produce a lot of noise and a lot of the townspeople began gathering to see what went on. The blaster himself was still cringing behind a building and waved them away, shouting, "Stay back, stay back, there are four more just like that."

So people learned, one from the other, often by sad or ludicrous experience, the many facets of their pioneer tasks.

WASHDAYS

Water for washing was hauled in barrels from the spring where we had first camped. The barrels were hauled on a stoneboat, a piece of board or small chunk of wood being put in each barrel to eliminate some of the splashing, they were then covered with burlap sacks and a washtub inverted over the top.

We used to haul the barrels in the wagon at first but the height of the wagon made this inconvenient and at first opportunity a large fork of tree branch was obtained. A chain was fastened to the main trunk as a place to hitch to, planks were nailed across the forked limbs and a durable and useful sledge resulted.

Everyone has probably read enough about the old washboiler and tin tub to picture the washday procedure, but a couple of things that might be of interest were: our washing machine, which was a covered, oblong tank. The lid held a set of cup-shaped plungers operated by a handle. Work the handle back and forth and the plungers worked up and down, agitating the clothes. A big improvement over this was what I think was called a vacuum washer. Just a funnel-shaped piece of heavily tinned metal on a stick handle. Plunge that up and down in your washing and you could really do a good job.

WASHDAYS

Some people had a wooden tub affair in which the agitator looked like a three-legged milk stool and was operated by turning a crank or large wheel.

To begin with, you had to have water and in most places that meant getting it the day before, from whatever available source. If you were affluent enough to have a horse, a stoneboat and a couple of barrels, you hauled the water to someplace near the kitchen and left it there for the next morning. It might be frozen with a two-inch coating of ice in the morning, but you had it handy. As soon as the morning fire got going in the cookstove, the old copper washboiler was set on the back of the stove to start heating while breakfast cooked: Breakfast out of the way, the boiler moved forward to better heat and a tub of rinse water moved into its place. All this providing you actually had an adequate supply of water: If you didn't have enough water you melted snow, and it takes a lot of snow to make enough water for a washing.

We all know about the old scrubboard routine and even see it pictured sometimes, but nobody quite pictures hanging out the finished product on the line at maybe ten below, when the thinner garments begin to stiffen and crackle before you even get the clothespin set. Eastern Montana nearly always had a breeze or even a gale, so the long-legged underwear and the overalls stood out stiff legged at an angle of thirty to forty degrees. Cold enough weather seemed to have a drying effect enough so that the clothes could be brought in in small installments and finish the drying near the stoves as time or space permitted.

Fuel wasn't something that you just tossed in the stove offhand, either. The wood hauled from however far, chopped and carried in. If you had coal, you dug and hauled it yourself, also from however far and you gave sincere thanks if there was an adequate supply.

It was on one of these washdays that one handle of the washboiler gave way as Lorna was lifting it off the stove. A cascade of scalding water flew up burning the entire left side of her face and breast, neck and shoulder. Picture to yourself the care and hospitalization such an injury would entail now and then picture her first coating the burn with a paste of soda to alleviate the initial pain and then smearing it with lard and going on about her household duties. There just wasn't anything else to do. There was a family of little kids to care for an no one else there to care for them. She was a horrible sight for a long time and then as the burn healed, new skin appeared, smooth and beautiful with a texture almost like a baby's skin. If any commercial beauty treatment could produce such results the women would beat down the doors.

I don't remember just when or what year the Morrow family moved off the claim; it was after child number five had died. A beautiful, golden haired little girl, she was stricken with appendicitis and was gone it seemed almost overnight. There were no antibiotics or any of our miracle medicines. If your appendix ruptured, you were going to need the constitution of a goat combined with a lot of luck to survive.

HORSEBITES AND RATTLESNAKES

The rumble of a large herd of running horses is truly an awe-inspiring sound, and, once heard, is not forgotten. The area where we settled was horse country and not frequented by many cattle. We used to see the herds, guarded and driven by the stallion at various times but they stayed well away from habitation if at all possible, wild and wary as antelope, at the first sight of a rider, the stallion would gather his herd and drive them to the top of the nearest hill where they could keep watch. Any laggard was given a nip that inspired an earnest desire to be at the very head of the herd.

Never underestimate the bite of a horse; a stallion can bite clear through the neck of a grown horse or tear out a lion-sized chunk of flesh. They can tear the cantle off a saddle, or pick up a man and shake him like a rag doll. Colts that were unable to keep up with the herd were sometimes grabbed and killed with one bite and shake. The mares kept between their colts and the stallion, hurrying them along and lashing out viciously if he came too near in trying to drive them faster.

When a stallion charges, he comes with head close to the ground; a determined-looking trot at first and then a savage rush designed to carry through in spite of any opposition. Aspiring young males might travel with the herd, keeping well in the clear and on the outskirts of the herd. The stallion would often graze innocently for half an hour or more, gradually working closer until within range, then charge with a slashing nip that kept the rival at a discrete distance for some time to come.

In spite of all the chilling stories about rattlesnakes we had heard before coming to Montana, I can't recall that any of us ever found one on our particular place. One of the horses was bitten in the nose. Its head swelled to huge proportions before it finally recovered, but we just didn't have many snakes. Other areas nearby had them, to be sure, and in some places there were lots of them but I wandered the hills or turned up rocks for two or three years before even seeing one. There was a weed that gave off a rattle that sounds similar to a snake and it gave me many a start but when I heard the real article there was no doubt in my mind.

There were the sites of old Indian camps to be found, indicated by the rings of stones which had been used to hold down the edges of the teepees. These were always some distance from water, perhaps in order not to alert game or to be out of sight of chance travelers. Sometimes a little promontory with a ledge of rock and a good view of the surrounding country would have little chips of flint and broken pieces of arrowheads. The worker in flint evidently acted as lookout for game or enemies as he carried on his arrowhead business. A man sitting almost motionless on a rock ledge would be practically invisible at even a short distance and would have the advantage of seeing any moving object long before being observed himself.

There was evidently some sort of organized trade in flint and jasper or, in fact, any type of conchoidal stone, since quarry pits have been found as well as caches of the rough stone where the trader had hidden it on his way to the area of his customers; also deposits of what is called preforms; that is, the stone was chipped into a sort of standard form which might be used as a scraper as it was, sharpened a little more for a knife or dressed to arrowhead size. This working of stone seems to have been a thing of a long time ago and not so recent as we usually suppose. We found some beautifully worked specimens at times, giving them away to visitors or sending them to friends without much thought of their actual history.

There were fascinating patterns of leaves, ferns and shells in many of the rocks. Beds of clay or sand sometimes held layers of shells or shiny jointed segments that looked like small

segments of lizards or snakes. Some mounds of clay and sandstone would hold hundreds of small balls of stone the size of
marbles or tennis balls. In the sides of cutbanks there were
sometimes large nodules of iron ore and I spent hours digging
in the hope of finding a mine of some sort. Now we are finding that certain areas in the sea cause various metals to pre-
cipitate from the water and collect in this fashion. How I would
have enjoyed having some of the books that are available now.
The children now have the books but all too few ever get to
actually see what they read about.

The small igloo nests of the meadowlark were common,
as well as the horned lark, the bobolink, the kildeer and the
nighthawk. Families of sharp-tailed grouse and sage hen
bobbed through the grass like tiny bits of brown fluff and disappeared like magic and I learned to imitate the mother's call
to assemble the flock.

There was a large band of sheep in the area, attended by
a Mr. Stewart. Whenever we had the chance to visit with him
we would try to find out more about the lay of the land, the
climate or any other information he could give us about the
country as he had been herding in that area for the previous
ten years. I think the sheep belonged to the Pope ranch somewhere toward Fallon.

THE STRANGE LIGHT

Our questioning of Mr. Stewart brought up a subject that
has remained a mystery to me all the years since,
although at the time we thought very little about it. He

stated that in the ten years he had been herding there, he had often seen a strange light that he couldn't explain. At that time, of course, no one was wandering around at night with a light and people were scarce at any time. His description brought on the usual explanation of swamp gas or St. Elmo's fire together with a bit of good-natured chaffing about having had one too many on his last trip to town, but he insisted that this was something different and soon avoided the subject.

Mr. Stewart's report was more or less forgotten for several years, but "Uncle Johnny" Conlon, with his propensity for getting lost, claimed that he had kept close watch of the neighbor's light on his way home and still found himself completely turned around. One night, when he could clearly see the Docken's light, he saw what he thought was someone walking with a lantern on top of a rocky hill quite near him. He called and the light went out. Uncle Johnny, superstitious as he was, lost no time in getting to his destination and told his story. This brought on far worse chaffing than Mr. Stewart had encountered, as Conlon's superstitions were well-known and all felt free to josh him.

All this ran on until the days of Model T cars with their dim lights and to a time when there were more people which might be on the roads at night. One night our neighbor, Frank Roberts, met what he thought was a dim car light coming down the road and turned out for it, but the light went over his car and went out. Frank was not a person given to excitement or exaggeration but he was truly puzzled and explained his experience to the neighbors. From then on we began to take more notice of any light we happened to see and tried to find some explanation or cause for it.

Whatever this phenomenon is, it is a fairly common occurrence, and the usual answers simply do not hold water, as it was seen at various locations covering an area of several square miles, winter or summer. It would vary in intensity from very dim to as bright as a fairly good car light, go up or down several feet, stand still or travel quite rapidly, change direction and travel against the prevailing breeze. This doesn't fit the ordinary answer and has always puzzled me. I saw it several times but never got close enough to get any better answer. We heard later that there was a similar occurrence in the Glendive area. Where there are lots of people, such things could easily go unnoticed, but in those first days, there were few lights and people just didn't go around on the prairie carrying lanterns; they mostly knew where they were going or let a horse do the piloting. Your guess is as good as anybody else's, think about it.

MAKING BUTTER

The summer of 1912 saw a lot of construction at our place. A large log bunkhouse was built, where we boys had our quarters and which provided extra room for guests. A large dugout and log cowbarn was made and a root cellar dug for the storage of vegetables and the cooling of milk. This was no sooner done than it was apparent that another root cellar would be necessary for storage of turnips for the stock.

Our turnip crop is something you are going to find hard to believe. We had planted the seed at random in the rows of a cornfield as there wasn't very much plowed land to begin with and we were doubtful whether the turnips would grow. We had rain every day in June that year and everything grew madly. The grass was lush and fairy rings of mushrooms were everywhere. By late summer we could see that we had turnips and lots of them but not until we began to pull them did we realize the size of the things. Imagine, if you can, a twenty-one pound turnip. We raised one, along with a number of eighteen pounders and loads of six or eight pounders. The storage root cellar was filled to the brim.

Dad went to Minnesota to buy stock that fall and took one of these specimens along with him. I think he took an eighteen pounder so that he wouldn't be just displaying the very biggest. He said it was cut in two to be sure it wasn't hollow and then put on display in the bank window.

That thin, tremendously rich layer which we saw with the first breaking of sod would have grown anything that moisture and temperature permitted.

Everyone who had any surplus at all sold butter or eggs in order to obtain a little cash or to use as credit against the grocery bill. These were the first item of crop or produce that any of the settlers had and everybody needed to make their farm start paying. Mother took particular pains to see that all eggs were clean and fresh when sold or we didn't sell any. Butter was worked until every bit of moisture was out of it and it was near the same color at all times as possible, and the cream that went into its production was carefully tended. It wasn't long until the store had standing orders for her produce. We found that butter was being sold as her product and so started the practice of signing each wrapper.

Today we more or less take butter for granted and few actually know just what real procedure is entailed in its production. Sure, you put cream in a churn or any other container, agitate it long enough and out comes—butter? Yes, small granules and lumps of butter, mixed with buttermilk, and of most any shade from standard butter color to almost white. Before you even start, the cream should be well cared for. It can be sour and in fact should not be absolutely fresh but there is a vast difference between sour and rancid.

Once the granules of butter are formed, the buttermilk is drained off and then the butter worked vigorously with a paddle to force out all the little drops of remaining moisture. Here again the customer can get a poor product or pay for water.

To facilitate this working process we got a contraption about three feet long and twenty inches wide with a serrated roller which ran back and forth on a rack to work the butter. It was a nice piece of maple construction but no good for its intended purpose, and the old hand paddle remained.

THE ROAD TO THE DEVIL

The first time we drove to Ismay, a town fourteen miles to the Southeast, we were amazed at the bustle and affluence of the place. The Erlingburt store was a large brick building which even had offices upstairs and it carried a stock of goods equal to that of a regular department store. Change baskets whizzed on their wires to the cashier's office just as they did in city stores, and wagons were at the loading platform loading up whole loads of supplies.

I think there was a bank and drugstore at that time also, and altogether it seemed a thriving little city in miniature. My clearest recollection is of the saloon; a small, false-fronted building, the false front was entirely taken up by a brightly painted sign, THE ROAD TO THE DEVIL. Some sign painter had really let his talent out for an airing in that case. The devil much resembled the one we used to see on the sacks of Red Devil cement. He was sitting up where he could keep good watch of a long, winding road, holding a trident like a three-pronged fish spear.

The saloon was operated then and for several years after by a Mr. Charles Degraffenreid, a former cowpuncher of the XIT ranch and it was just a quiet men's club where the ordinary fellow could have a glass of beer or sit down to rest or visit in peace, but the sign gave fair warning about any overindulgence. The name was soon changed to the Yellowstone Trail Bar but some years ago, when I last saw the place, the devil was still holding his own, his sturdy red beginning to show through the faded yellow of the later sign. I understand that the place is burned down now, but surely, somewhere, there must be a picture of that sign.

There was a large livery stable operated by another XIT alumni, a Mr. Bill Roberts. Bill lived in Ismay many years and raised his family there. He was later to give one of the champion rodeo riders his first start toward recognition and fame.

THE ROAD TO THE DEVIL

Some time in the fall of 1912 the people of the neighborhood began gathering at the schoolhouse once or twice a month to discuss better methods of farming or mutual problems that had arisen. The women brought lunch, huge pots of coffee were brewed on the heating stove and everyone got a chance to visit more than any of them had had time to before. It was the beginning of what was to be called the community club. Later a community hall would be built, a baseball team formed, picnics held and all the rest, but now they were just beginning.

It was at one of these first meetings that a young county extension agent came from Miles City which was the county seat. This young man must have been just out of school and perhaps the first of his kind, for he surely knew nothing of the problems confronting his audience. His main theme was the need for shelter belts of trees and he could see no reason why people hadn't planted them. Each home should be surrounded by a large grove of trees. The grownups maintained a stolid silence but some of us younger fry were rude enough to snicker. He rather icily explained that those who had never lived anywhere else of course couldn't appreciate the value of trees. We never saw him again, as he probably gave us up as a lost cause, but the next agent knew what he was talking about or if not he was trying to learn, for he ran a farm of his own, experimenting, as was everyone else, to find out what would grow or what could be used as a cash crop in this new land.

Every one of the families represented at that first meeting with the county agent had transplanted trees, carefully nurtured them and carried buckets of water to them only to see them rejected by a soil which simply refused to raise trees or scorched by a sun that baked the earth. This, in spite of the fact that it had been a wet summer.

PICNICS AND COUNTRY BOX SOCIALS

There was need of a well at the school for we had carried water from Mr. McAtee's well some quarter of a mile away. A well driller was contacted and came with his rig, getting an adequate supply of soft, good tasting water. This was cause for celebration by all concerned and a community picnic was scheduled. Lafe Young, coffee-loving Norwegian that he was, volunteered to make the coffee, for some of the coffee at the other gatherings just hadn't been up to his standard and he wanted things to be the very best for this occasion. Picnic day arrived and Lafe set up a washboiler on a foundation of rocks, measured water and coffee grounds meticulously and tended his fire with knowing care. Just before time for lunch, Lafe, Dad and a few other coffee experts decided to make the final test. What had looked all right in the washboiler assumed a greenish hue in the cup and tasted awful. The water contained soda and no amount of doctoring would make good coffee from it. Poor Lafe was a long time hearing the last of that day.

The usual country box socials were held to raise money for different projects and we are all familiar with the routine of them so there was nothing unusual. Dad had a good carrying voice and so was elected to be auctioneer. This was the start of a number of real auctioneering jobs for him in later years.

The masquerade dance is not normally different, usually, but two of them brought some real talent. One was held in the

Cabin Creek district about ten miles east of our town. Now beautiful and charming young ladies were a scarce article and a new one which nobody had ever seen before was a sensation. One appeared at this dance with high heels, a low cut dress and a string of pearls that all the young fellows admired greatly. She danced beautifully and flirted primly but when the masks came off, so did a wig, revealing an impishly smiling young man.

The other dance was held at Mildred and the star performer there was a fellow who faced both ways: That is, he had sewn the front half of matching suits and shoes together for his costume. By walking stiffly as an automaton, and perhaps by dancing with one or two partners who were in on the secret, he seemed to go in either direction with equal facility. He finally was detected by one of his masks slipping enough to reveal an ear. How many hours of sewing and practice must have gone into his preparation!

Amusement was scarce then and a practical joker might spend weeks carefully laying up the background for some straight-faced bit of tomfoolery to be sprung on an unsuspecting friend.

TRAPPING AND HUNTING

Trapping was always the farm boy's main source of income and as soon as he was old enough to wander by himself at all he began dreaming of easy fortune. Any farm magazine had the advertisements of fur companies and at times there were pictures of catches which would have spelled a vast treasure to any boy.

HOMESTEADING

There were muskrats in the creeks, weasels, hunted mice and rabbits along the bottomland brushpatches, once in a while there were the tracks of bobcats and sometimes a den of skunks might be found.

We watched the rise and fall of fur prices and the changes of fashion as they concerned furs as avidly as young brokers watching the stock market. What matter if our entire catch for the year might only total five or six dollars? Five or six dollars or five or six million are all the same if it's all you've got.

Muskrats brought from fifteen cents to as much as a dollar, weasels about seventy-five cents, and skunks as much as two or three dollars. A den of skunks could mean real affluence. Then, of course, there was the coyote. Here was the grand prize that might even reach ten dollars. It took a skill far beyond the ability of the average farm boy to catch one but it was the shining goal of all young trappers.

There was still an occasional wolf in the district, but the idea of getting one of them compared to the present day Reader's Digest Grand Prize: It might even happen to you, but ... The stockmen's association usually paid one hundred dollars bounty for the scalp of any wolf and if the animal had gained any fame as a stock-killer, the various ranchers in his particular range would supplement this reward with contributions of their own, varying with the extent of their losses. Some twenty generations of intensive harassment had produced a wary and sagacious animal that was more than a match for the most experienced 'wolfer,' as the men were called who had professionally hunted wolves in earlier days. I will describe one of them and his methods later.

TRAPPING AND HUNTING

Trapping, even when done by an expert, is the epitome of cruelty: Done by the amateur, it is still worse, and yet I know of no surer way for a boy to gain the knowledge of animals and the kinship with them that one gains in trapping. To have a coyote steal the bait from your set, calmly scratch between your traps and leave the unmistakable mark of his utter contempt for your wiles is the beginning of a lifetime of respect and study of all so-called dumb animals.

We had brought traps for small game such as muskrat and skunk but had none large enough for coyote, and, for the beginner, the investment of three or four dollars in coyote traps seemed like sheer folly. Reasoning that by doubling the spring power of one of the smaller traps I could improvise one strong enough for my purpose, I set about filing the frame of one until it would accept a second spring. With this makeshift, I felt ready for big business. I had seen Mr. Stewart, the herder, setting coyote traps and gathered as much of his advice as possible, learning that he wore new cotton gloves in handling the traps in order to avoid any human scent, used a sheepskin to stand on while setting the traps, stepping on it as he got off his horse, and that he covered the traps with fine soil and grass to make everything look natural. He admitted to using a bait which he manufactured himself, but such recipes were the treasured secrets of the expert and not revealed any more readily than would be the secret of some hidden gold mine.

I set my homemade coyote trap with all the care I could muster, laying the dirt aside on a piece of paper as I dug the place for the trap and carrying away the surplus when I had covered everything flush with the ground. I had placed a piece of meat under the trap in the hope that a coyote would dig for it and be caught. Somehow, in spite of all my care, the ground didn't look natural there, but it was the best I could do. The days went slowly by, seemingly without end, but finally something, I couldn't tell what, had dug up my trap, turning it over without springing it and stolen the bait. At least I had nearly caught something but it seemed more likely that a badger had upset my plans. I could see that the idea of putting bait under the trap was likely to bring the same result again but didn't know of any better way. Finally, the day came when the trap was sprung. The chain was pulled out straight from its stake and there were a few short yellowish hairs clinging to the jaws of the trap. I had actually nipped a coyote! The thought never occurred to me that it was, beyond doubt, a young pup, as inept at his business as I was at mine. I hope his lesson in caution served him well throughout a long and hearty life, for he gave me one of the greatest thrills of my boyhood. It would be a long time before I at last trapped a coyote and when I looked into those unflinching yellow eyes there was no sense of elation, but the feeling of having failed or betrayed an old friend.

The coyote has adapted himself to all the changes since that time, thriving on adversity and outwitted man almost to the point of endangering his own environment. I hear his youngsters practice their chorus in the fall evenings, hear him call to his friends across the canyon and laugh his derision at the town dogs. I admire him.

I know very little about the wolves but will try to piece together the bits of information that have come my way over the years; there seems to have been two distinct types of wolf:

TRAPPING AND HUNTING

The first, which some of the ranchers call a lobo, must have been a native of the country and ranged in size about halfway between the coyote and the gray wolf. He doesn't seem to have been regarded as much of a stock killer but was soon eliminated by the traps, hounds and poisons of the stockmen. The other wolf, the gray, which might vary in color from almost white to black, was, I think, what we now call the Siberian wolf.

During the days of the slaughter of buffalo for hides, the wolves had increased to a large number: Then, when the buffalo were gone and cattle began to come in, their population dropped precipitously. True, the cattlemen began hunting them and hired professional wolfers, but there was a good bit of speculation as to what had caused such a rapid decline. Game biologists have found that wolves will limit the size of their families to the amount of food available. If game becomes scarce, they will kill one or more pups until the family is of a size that can be adequately fed.

With the coming of cattle, the wolf was hunted by every available means. Nearly all riders carried guns and ropes. The professional trappers turned to the wolfing trade and carcasses of stock were poisoned, so that soon only the most wary animals survived. The pups learned the lessons taught by their elders and the slow or unwise of their generation fell victim to the hunters, so in the twenty or more years of the cattle area, there developed a creature that only the expert or the very lucky was able to catch.

Several years after leaving Eastern Montana, I had the pleasure of meeting and questioning a man who had been the last professional wolfer and probably the most successful one in that area. He told me that the wolves would have one path to approach their den and another which they used in leaving. In setting traps in these paths, the trapper had to be sure that nothing was changed or disturbed. The displacement of a single stick or stone along these paths would cause the wolves to move their den. They would also move if the trapper was seen in the vicinity of the den.

I was told of one instance where this hunter located a family of two old wolves and five pups. He studied all their movements as the summer progressed, learning their routes of travel, the times they might be expected in certain areas and all the information he could possibly gather about their habits; of course as the pups became grown wolves, their depredations increased and additional rewards were offered to supplement the regular bounty. When he considered the time right for the harvest, the wolfer chose his field of fire and was waiting for the pack one morning. He got five of them there and killed the other two shortly afterward. That was the kind of patience and observation necessary to hunt wolves successfully.

I was particularly interested to learn of his method in trailing wolves. I had often heard of riders running them down, and asked him about it. He explained that occasionally someone did run one down by coming upon the wolf when it had just gorged itself on beef or when there was the opportunity to obtain relays of fresh horses, but these cases were an exception rather than the rule. He stated that he seldom rode faster than a walk or jog-trot, in this way not alarming the wolf into precipitous flight: The wolf would circle and watch his back track, becoming worried when he was sure he was being followed, and yet wanting to keep in touch with his pursuer.

He stated that he nearly always got the wolf within two or three days and described his pursuit of the last wolf which he

TRAPPING AND HUNTING

got in that area. He said that on the evening of the second day he saw the wolf watching him from a little knoll and felt sure he could have shot it but was not sure what was on the other side of the hill, so waited until the next day to get his game.

Hihram Brackett had been a buffalo hunter in that area in the early days and when the buffalo were gone had worked as a wolfer, then when disaster began to overtake the cattlemen he bought a band of sheep and hired a Mexican herder to care for them.

Cattlemen killed the herder and scattered the sheep but Mr. Brackett purchased a good stock of supplies, plenty of ammunition for his old buffalo rifle, moved his band of sheep to a large flat, set up camp and sent word to the cattlemen that he was there and would be pleased to have anyone try to dislodge him. He was a white-haired old gentleman when we first came to Montana and lived well into his eighties. I used to pester him to tell me of the game in the buffalo hunting days. He mentioned killing an elk along the creek bottom just north of Ismay, and of forgetting to take the ramrod out of his rifle while shooting at a buffalo and blowing up the gun. This happened just across the creek to the West of Ismay. I mention these incidents to give some idea of his experience in the area. I have no idea when Mr. Brackett first came to Montana or where his original home was. I do know that at his ranch there was an oak chair with a coat of arms carved on it. Whatever of heraldry and knighthood that coat of arms represented, Mr. Brackett upheld with honor. All who knew him liked and respected him.

The Brackett ranch was about eight miles South of our claim, and when we first homesteaded the family must have been there for a good many years. Mrs. Brackett had educated their three daughters there on the ranch, preparing them for college and they had gone through college with ease. There had been a son who drowned while swimming in a reservoir at the ranch. One of the daughters was my teacher in third or fourth grade.

Mrs. Brackett never sat down to read without the dictionary within easy reach. She read only the best literature or articles available and if there was the least doubt in her mind about the pronunciation or meaning of a word she looked it up right then and there. The Brackett family were always the supporters of any worthwhile project for the community and I feel privileged to have known them.

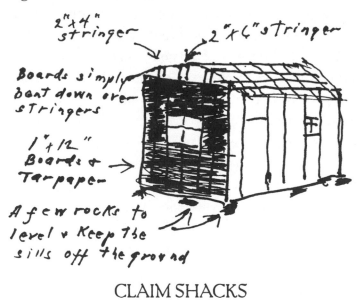

CLAIM SHACKS

This is the 12' x 14' claim shack which sprang up almost overnight. I have exaggerated the roof stringers and the curve of the roof in order to give a little better idea of the way the things were constructed. There were a number of reasons why this particular plan was used: First, it was cheap and the whole thing could be hauled in one load. Second, by getting twelve and fourteen foot lengths of lumber, there was practically no waste material and almost no sawing. One man with a hammer, nails and saw could build his house and be living in it in a day or two, depending on his skill. That matter of time and skill was a big factor. It takes know-how to frame rafters, but anybody can somehow nail down a 2x6 placed on edge for a stringer down the center of the building, position a couple of 2x4s the same way and bend boards over them to nail to the plate. Cover the whole building with tarpaper and set up housekeeping in just about as depressing an edifice as men ever contrived.

We read about the sod shanty but seldom ever get to see one. A properly built sod house can be a cosy and comfortable home, warm in winter and cool in summer. With a good coat of whitewash on the inner walls and ceiling, you have a shining white room. Here again the element of time and skill came into play. It takes time to plow and haul sod for a house. It takes skill to choose the proper sod and to lay up the tapering walls, much thicker at the bottom than at the top, placing the sods as a bricklayer lays up his bricks.

Many of the early Norwegian settlers in Dakota Territory built sod houses because lumber was not available and also most of them were skilled workmen at some sort of manual construction, but the homesteaders in our area were of a different category, many of them having no practical experience in building or even rural living.

The 12' by 14' shack was mainly the trademark of the fellow who planned to stay only long enough to prove up on his claim, hoping to sell to latecomers who really wanted to make a home. As the years went by, these little shacks were hauled away to be used as granaries, hen houses, and incorporated into more substantial homes as additional rooms. There are peat modern homes today that still contain vestiges of some old claim shack, its boards brittle and hard with age.

A young couple with a new baby moved in and built one of the 12' by 14' shacks on the Little Whitney Creek, not far from the Alex McDonald ranch. I don't even know their name or when they arrived, but it was probably early summer because they had just got the house built and a little patch of garden plowed or spaded when the baby died and they gave up and moved away.

The last time I saw the place, stock had trampled and smashed the little porch, broken through the floor and rubbed down part of the fence around the baby's grave. The creek was undercutting the bank and would soon swallow up both grave and house.

So many high hopes and dreams ended in tragedy and the sites of the homesteads have vanished like the teepee rings of the Indians.

ALEX McDONALD'S VISITOR

Mr. McDonald had been on his ranch on the Little Whitney Creek for twenty years and as I remember it he had six or eight stacks of old hay which had been a surplus in some mild winter and so were no good for stock feed. Some of these stacks were bought for making the barn roof and the roofs of later cattle sheds.

ALEX McDONALD'S VISITOR

When you approached the Alex McDonald ranch you got an impression of antiseptic cleanliness and order that I am unable to picture or describe. The first impression didn't even begin to prepare you for the real fact. I have never known anyone, man or woman, so meticulously neat, clean and orderly in every way as Mr. McDonald.

The house roof had been made by laying corrugated sheet iron over the ridge poles and covering it with a layer of crushed scorio rock which is about the dark red color of the Spanish type tile we see nowadays. The eaves extended out about two feet from the walls to provide shade. There was a flock of sharp-tailed grouse that used to come each afternoon to be fed and to rest in the shade near the house. These grouse will normally come to water about one or two o'clock in the afternoon and then seek the shade of buffalo berry bushes or plum thickets until about five o'clock or until the heat of the sun has abated. Here there were buffalo thickets and the shade of ash, box-elder and cottonwood trees along the creek about a hundred yards from the house, but these birds came like tame pets for their little treat and the companionship of man.

The yard surrounding the house was raked and the paths swept until there was not a twig or blade of grass misplaced. The fences, the haystacks, the corrals and everything about the place continued this orderliness until one caught themselves wondering whether the wind had ever blown or a storm come to disrupt the scene.

Disruption had come at one time, however, and in a most revolting form: Alex had just made his fall trip to Terry, some thirty miles away, for his winter's supply of sugar, flour, dried fruits, etc. Such a trip takes two days; one day to get there, put up your team, visit with the storekeeper as you choose what clothing you're going to need from what he has available then give him the long list of groceries that you've compiled during several weeks. As time permits that evening, the grocer lays out the pile of supplies to be ready for you in the morning.

The second day of his trip, Alex loaded his wagon and went home, arriving late in the evening. He unloaded his supplies in a pile against one wall of his one-room home to be stored away neatly later.

The following morning required a check on the stock that would entail most of a full day's ride and it was while he was gone that a traveller came to the ranch. When he found no one at home, the stranger followed the time-honored custom of the country and made himself at home.

He cooked his meal, set his place neatly at what would be the guest's spot at the little table and ate his dinner. After dinner he rolled a smoke and leaned back to relax as men will always do. This position left him facing the door. Leaning back must have brought his gaze upward to a shotgun hanging over the doorway, the standard place for guns in those days. He got a splinter of wood from the woodbox, took down the gun, placed the muzzle in his mouth and pushed the trigger with the stick of wood.

When Alex returned, he made the long trip to Terry that night, then the return trip the next day with the deputy in his buckboard buggy.

After the investigation and the removal of the body, Alex threw out all his pile of supplies and spent most of the night scrubbing the place. When he finally gave up for some rest, he considered the house at least clean enough for the time being. However: "There was one of his dommed eyes, right in the very middle of my bed." Concussion had blown this item clear across the room and away from the rest of the mess.

McDonald also had a summer camp about two miles from his main ranch. I have never understood just why another house was so near the home ranch except that mosquitoes may have been a nuisance at times along the creek bottoms and hay meadows in the early summer. At any rate, this house was kept with equal neatness. The path to the spring, about seventy yards away was kept swept. The stove was polished to a glistening black and every time he added a stick of wood, Alex would dust off the top of the stove with a goosewing. The goosewing itself was cleaner than when the goose wore it. As the visitor went out the door, Alex automatically swept along behind him. Twenty years of neatness had become unconscious reflex.

One day Mr. McDonald came visiting. He was dressed in his best, which consisted of pants that were bleached nearly white with washing and bound at the cuff with red and yellow cord, and a shirt starched so stiff that it nearly creaked. He seemed preoccupied, as though he had something on his mind which he was reluctant to bring forth. He stayed visiting with Mother until the rest of us had left and then produced the picture of a boyhood sweetheart in Scotland, confiding that they were going to be married.

The new Mrs. McDonald proved to be a fine looking lady with blue-black hair, blue eyes and altogether a splendid sort of person. They lived on the ranch for about three years, had a little daughter and later moved into town so that Mrs. McDonald might have companionship. Alex operated the livery stable and dray line for a while in order to have something to do.

The disorder and squalor of that little town must have been a hardship to them both, however, as Mrs. McDonald was the equal of Alex in cleanliness if not in fussiness about her housekeeping. We lost track of them when they moved from town. They probably returned to Scotland.

EXPLORERS, AUTOMOBILES AND THE PHONOGRAPH

The community sawmill was only operated for a matter of a few weeks at most. There was not much suitable timber and so far as I know no heed was paid to whose land the timber might be growing on. Each member involved in the project got a few loads of lumber for his immediate building needs and then probably the man who acted as sawyer, a Mr. Wade, must have bought the shares of the other partners and moved the saw somewhere else.

Dad acted as cook, since he had at one time cooked on the roundup crews in Dakota. I am glad to see that the dutch oven is coming back into popularity, for the cook who can really use one can produce the tastiest of meals. Stews, steaks, roasts, biscuits or pudding, all seemed to come from one or two of those big iron kettles and all done to perfection. Maybe the smell of pine, sage and freshly cut lumber had a lot to do with it.

While cutting timber, one of the Striker boys found the skeleton of a man. The left temple had been bashed in. The man had not been killed by a fall from a horse, as there were no articles such as spurs lying about. Probably some herder killed by cattlemen or the settling of some old grudge left over from the Johnson County War. We were not a great distance from the area where this trouble took place and it was then, and still is, a touchy subject.

I don't mean to imply in any way that there were conditions such as we see pictured in the present day shows. There was far more courtesy and consideration of the other fellow's rights than we see now, generally, but the people were strong-minded individuals; shall we say, bullheaded? At times they were, and people will still quarrel.

Whatever, the bones were left as they were found and after a couple of years more the porcupines and other rodents must have disposed of them.

I don't know just how or have the words to describe our communication or lack of it up to and even through the First World War. There were a few in the community who couldn't read and a few others about as highly educated as the ordinary person ever got in those times without some sort of specialization.

This was a time of change and adventure. We followed the explorations of Amundson and Cook, speculating as to the usefulness of their effort and risk. From our own experience we knew the effects of even moderate exposure and cold. When Cook and his men were at last found so near to safety it seemed somehow a national failure or tragedy; tragedy it was, and there seemed to be unrest or trouble everywhere. There were revolutions in Cuba and Mexico, there were wars and massacres in the Balkan countries and we saw our own country dabbling in affairs that seemed to us very far afield.

The automobile was beginning to be useful but such a thing as a truck was only used on good roads. The airplane could fly or at least get off the ground; we even had a snapshot of one which a friend had seen flying at some exhibition, but the idea of them ever being commercially useful seemed impossible. I even remember reading some science article about how an earth satellite might stay in orbit if it could be sent high enough.

Any publication one got was of course covering news or events which were out of date. No radio, no T.V., no news reels and in most places no movies.

One gets a picture of a mental vacuum and yet I sometimes wonder whether the ordinary person wasn't more accurately informed than we are today, for this reason: Even though a man might not read, he was glad of the chance to discuss any news and his long periods of solitude gave him ample time to mull over in his mind what he had been told. The settler who got any magazine with editorials, and there were some good ones, had a week or even a month to go through his reading word for word and long hours on the plow or at his work gave him time to weigh each item carefully. This, with the leavening of those who were educated or had battled their way to political influence resulted in a pretty high level of common sense. There wasn't the amount of class isolation that we have now. The banker, the rancher, and the down and outer might all be found chatting on some sunny bench, not bosom pals, any of them, but all the same they were getting the other fellows' viewpoints.

The family who read a chapter of the Bible every night, the old gentleman who studied Gibson's "Decline and Fall of The Roman Empire," the part-time cowpuncher who had a library of good authors in his one-room shack, or the sheep-

EXPLORERS, AUTOMOBILES AND THE PHONOGRAPH

herder who spent most of his wages for books on philosophy were all very much inclined to turn over the stones of news to see what sort of worm lay hidden beneath the surface.

Dad was a very good reader and it was our custom to choose one continued story which he would read aloud for us. The rest of our stories we had to read for ourselves unless we had some difficulty. How we used to hustle through the chores on the nights we got the magazines! We subscribed to *The Youth's Companion, The Saturday Evening Post, The Popular Magazine, The Dakota Farmer* and received back issues of *Harper's* and other good magazines from relatives. Close neighbors formed the habit of subscribing to different publications so that they could exchange with their friends.

Music was something that our own immediate community lacked. Almost every household had some sort of instrument in the hope that one of the children would learn to play or that someone would come visiting who was a musician. A family by the name of Lewis finally moved in, settling on a place near the edge of the Pines; both of them played almost any stringed instrument and of course furnished music for dances, but as a general rule we were all sort of hungry for music and if one heard someone singing or whistling any classical tune it set them apart in your mind as having a better background somewhere in the past. Among some of the old ranches there had been a cosmopolitan society, with visitors or investors from France, England and Germany but these people were gone now and the ranches themselves were more a memory than substance. The winter of 1886-7 had broken the cattle business and turned away the financiers who backed many of the big ranches. The country dance was fine for an evening's entertainment, but there was a general longing for just plain music and the communion of listening or sharing of feeling that only good music can bring.

Uncle Johnny Conlon was the first one in our close vicinity who got a phonograph and, generous old soul that he was, he used to bring it with him whenever he came to visit for an evening. His choice of records left a whole lot to be desired, as his favorites were 'Uncle Josh' but some of them were music. There wasn't a great choice of records to be had. The Sousa marches were a popular item at the time, and the opera singers: Caruso, Gallicurci, Patti. But unless one understood Italian or knew the theme of the opera there wasn't much point in listening very long.

There had been a fad of popularity for operas and many people felt they had to listen to opera whether they cared for or understood it or not. It was the thing to do.

We were all grateful for Uncle Johnny's visits and spent many a pleasant evening listening to his records and just enjoying the company of someone outside our own family. It was on some of his visits about the neighborhood until late evenings that Mr. Conlon saw the mysterious lights that I mentioned before and spent much of his night finding his way home. I heartily wish now that we had taken some pains to investigate this phenomenon.

THE *TITANIC*

I don't even remember when the tragedy occurred, but it has always seemed to me that the sinking of the *Titanic* marked some sort of turning point in the attitude of people all over the country. There was a lot of speculation and talk about the whole affair, of course, and it seems to have brought a lot of doubts and questions or trends into focus. Here was a magnificent example of the best in engineering and workmanship, the very crest of the shipbuilding art, built to be unsinkable and the bottom was ripped out of it like a toy balloon. Here were some of the most legendary figures of our society and the political world swept away like the figures of a shadow play. Here was trusted and supposedly competent authority failing to heed timely warning or to act according to the dictates of common sense. As I remember the discussions now, that lack of common sense seemed to rankle most with ordinary people. The people of our own little community had been learning the hard way that common sense and timely precaution were a lot safer than setting up some record for speed.

There was another ship, the *Sussex*, that must have been sunk in something like the same period, possibly the start of the First World War, as I remember playing with two boats I had made and called the *Titanic* and the *Sussex*.

We used to get kerosene in five-gallon tins at times and it was by cutting and flattening two of these cans that I had made my boats; they were just canoe-shaped affairs and very crudely made, but would carry quite a cargo of rocks or sods from one side of a small pond to the other. By throwing rocks I could create storms or sink my ships at will, but it was always a matter of protocol for the *Titanic* to be sunk last.

The awareness of the outside world and the questioning of foreign events that was developing in my own mind must have been in some way paralleled in our whole society and the changes came so rapidly as to be only a confused jumble to me now. The great and the humble, the dolt and the wise, all seem to have been living in some sort of play world where everything would turn out for the best. Although some of the people had come from foreign countries, I think that even they felt that they were beyond reach of the tides of world events which would soon sweep over us all.

THE YELLOWSTONE TRAIL

The Yellowstone Trail must have been established in 1913, as I have the first road map, dated April, 1914, with apologies for lack of accurate information. Whatever the date, the thought of having a national highway through the area set us all to feeling that we were in the main stream of progress. Each little town wanted the highway right down their main street, and we hunted for long slabs of rock to be painted bright yellow and set up as trail markers.

Trail was the proper name for it, because that is all it was for a long time thereafter. As late as 1919, there was a place somewhere near the Tongue River that the road ran along, a level stretch that suddenly dived over the edge of a coulee with an almost right-angle turn at the very edge. I well remember the condition if not the exact location, because we narrowly missed having an accident there. We had passed through a stretch of bottomland thick with brush and trees, where the road wound around some blind curves and was only wide enough for one car. We met another car on one of these turns and both backed up to gain clearance enough to creep past, but the approach to this deathtrap was smooth straight road along level-looking prairie and we must have been zipping along at a full twenty-five miles an hour when a narrow coulee appeared as if by magic. The most dangerous curve of today looks very innocent in comparison but everyone was still used to the old team and wagon then so we expected any sort of surprise in the way of road.

It was along this same Yellowstone Trail that I once roped a pup coyote. Just as I was playing with the struggling pup and giving my horse a breather, along came a tourist and his wife. I don't know where they were from, but the sight of a kid with a roped coyote must have been quite a novelty to them, for the man slammed on the brakes and hopped out, pocketbook in hand, wanting to buy the pup. I wasn't too young to recognize easy pickings and named a price of five dollars, a fabulous sum. The only fly in the ointment was the wife. The second that wonderful five dollar bill appeared she flatly stated, "You aren't going to have that thing in the back of that car." End of dream and the man shamefacedly got in the car and drove off. He didn't know what a blessing his wife had conferred upon him because a coyote pup has to be caught very young, before he leaves the den, to ever become tame. From the time they are the size of a jackrabbit and have run around outside the den a bit, they are wild and want to stay that way.

Our neighbors, the Strikers, caught a very small pup, but still one which was running around outside the den and set about trying to make a pet of him. They made a fine den for him by digging a hole and covering it with a box full of dirt.

The pup soon learned to come out for food when the girls called him but spent his time hidden in his den for the most part. Before very long, there seemed to be less and less chickens around the place but no sign of what was happening to them. The pup had got so that he wouldn't even come out of his den to eat when food was put out for him so the girls sat quietly one day to watch him when he finally did come out to eat. The food dish remained untouched for some time and finally one of the hens discovered it and began to eat; that was when Puppy came out to eat, and in a flash of yellowish fur the hen and pup were both out of sight without so much as a squawk. When the cover was taken off his den, Puppy's cleverness was revealed by a fine bed of feathers, but he had been smart enough to keep his front door neat and clear of any evidence of his crimes.

I have seen one or two tame coyotes and as little fellows they will come running and wagging their tails like any other puppy, but as they grow older they seem aloof and reserved, more than a dog. However tame he may be, the coyote still has an extremely keen mind, a restless nature, and the dullness of domestication soon sets him to figuring ways to amuse himself or to add an occasional snack of poultry to his diet.

THE XIT RANCH

I have mentioned a couple of the men who worked for the XIT ranch and might as well give a bit of the background of this outfit, for there were still a lot of the fellows around who had worked together on the ranch at one time or another and they constituted a sort of fraternity much as buddies in the same outfit in the army. Many of the little happenings of that time concerned some of these men and their transition or lack of it from the cattle business to some other occupation was an integral part of our settlement.

Please forgive me if I seem to know more about their time than my age warranted, or if I get to writing as though I had any part in it, but I had three uncles who worked the Judith Basin area in the early eighties, who spoke of those times as though they were yesterday. They knew and worked with Charlie Russel when he worked as night wrangler for Prue's outfit, gone through the winter of '86-'87, which marked the end of the real cattle era. Dad had worked for ten years in the Dakota cattle business, we were trying to get started at ranching and our place was the stopping off spot for any of the ranchers or cowpunchers who happened to be going through the country. Like any other kid, I wanted to learn to ride and rope and I soaked up the shop-talk of these men. They were experts and authorities on the cattle business and all its fascinating background.

The XIT ranch, as a company, was formed by some Chicago financiers headed by a Mr. Farwell. These men were not affected by the romance of the cattle business, they were shrewd investors who knew a good thing when they saw it, using cattle as a stopgap while land values increased.

The state of Texas had land almost without limit and offered to trade acreage for the construction of a capitol building.

For this finance, the group received 3,050,000 acres of land, approximately ten counties, hence the XIT or ten in Texas.

They set about enclosing these holdings with the new barbed wire which required some six thousand miles of fence. Fences were highly unpopular in those days to the men who had been used to open range, and for a while the new management was considered fair game for rustlers, but the XIT brand proved to be something that wasn't easy to work over. The legend grew up that one rustler was offered his pardon if he would disclose how he changed the brand to a five pointed star and a cross. Try it some time. You'll find it quite a puzzle.

The management chose good foremen, good cooks for their roundup crews and brought in improved grades of stock. As it became recognized that stock could winter farther North they began grazing herds in that direction for the better range and to get away from ticks.

In 1890, probably taking advantage of a depressed market which hadn't recovered from the disastrous winter of '86-87, they bought a small ranch about sixty miles North of Miles City then leased two million acres between the Yellowstone and Missouri rivers, giving them a total holding of more than five million acres.

The first herd brought up from the Texas ranch numbered 10,000 head and as time went on, other herds were brought up.

The XIT ranch itself used to run two roundup wagons. There would be about twenty-five men to each crew. A good wagon boss and a good cook were the basis of a good crew. There would be from three to four wagons and crews from big outfits of other ranges come to get their stock, which during the year had drifted onto the XIT range; also there would be small ranches represented by two or three men apiece in the roundup, so at times there might be as many as 150 men gathering the cattle in one area.

The roundups were headed by the wagonboss of whatever ranch claimed the range being worked, and all mavericks were branded for that ranch, in this case, the XIT. The cattle gathered in the day were brought to one central location and segregated into different herds there each evening. Each crew might bring in as many as three thousand cattle. Cows with calves were separated into groups and the calves branded according to the brand of the mother. Herds were sorted according to ownership and each wagon took possession of its stock; some to be taken back to the home range and some to be shipped for beef.

In the fall beef roundup, the XIT shipped about two train loads of beef each week. The roundup wagon with its crew would take the week's gathering of beef to Miles City, Terry or Fallon to be shipped. On the following week the other crew would ship. Each wagon made as many as five shipments, so that's a lot of beef.

1906 was an extremely wet year and the winter of 1906-07 was a winter of deep snow, killing thousands of cattle. The loss of cattle through the hard winter and the influx of sheep saw about the last of the really big beef operations in the fall of 1907.

The men who had worked for the XIT and other big ranches were left pretty much as a shoemaker without a last. They were highly trained specialists at their trade, and most of their trade had disappeared.

The art of being a good stockman meant a lot more than just wearing riding boots; I will give two little examples, one as a beginner and the other as the finished product so that the reader can sort of test his own ability or aptitude. This is a day of aptitude tests anyway. First: As a kid I was appointed to check on some of the stock and took another kid friend along with me. About ten days later we made the same round again and he immediately began looking for more cattle, saying that some were missing and describing them. Here was the beginning of a born stockman; he knew and remembered those cattle as individuals after having ridden through the herd once. To me, they were just a bunch of cows, and I didn't even know that any were missing. For the second example: A friend of mine accompanied a cattle buyer on one of his trips; they rode through the herd and the buyer chose eighty head to be delivered to the yards. As they left the herd, the buyer wrote his estimated weight of these cattle on a slip of paper and handed it to my friend, saying that they would compare his guess with the actual weight when they were weighed out at the yards. He missed the true weight by ten pounds. What do you think of your own ability as a stockman?

Mr. Cato, who had managed the Montana part of XIT, bought out what was left and ran a still sizable ranch, also becoming sheriff of Custer County and a state senator.

Many of the men found work with the smaller ranches and some went to various other jobs but the old feeling of fellowship remained through the years.

Many of the men who wanted to continue their occupation as cowboys got work at small ranches and I'm sure were really better off, as the ranchers now realized that their stock must be fed through the winters and began hiring year-round help.

Some of the names I recall were: Bill Fought, Steve Macomber, Charlie Clements, Si Robinson and J.K. Marsh. Mr. Marsh had somehow acquired the nickname of Buger Face John Marsh: Perhaps at some time when he was a kid he had bugered his face, that is, scratched or bruised it in some accident, and someone began calling him that to tease him or to distinguish him from all other Johns. However he got the nickname, he was a nice-looking man with the most kindly of faces. Everybody who knew him liked him. These men worked at various times and were frequent visitors at the Buckley and Renn ranches some thirty miles Northeast of our home. Claude McCracken is another name which just came to mind. All of them top hands with stock.

The Renn ranch wasn't what we would call small now as one pasture near the home place contained ten thousand acres. The Renn brothers, Paul, Carl and Ed were from Germany, well educated and fine musicians. Carl said once that he and his brothers arrived in Montana in the fall with five dollars between them to get through the winter. I don't know when they arrived, probably around 1890, because they had a well-established ranch in the early 1900s. Paul had made and lost two sizable fortunes and was well on his way to a third at the time of his death. The ranch is still operated by his son Paully.

Frank Buckley must have come into the country in the late 90s, coming West for his health, as he faced a threat of tuberculosis. Mr. Buckley and his ranch were both in very robust condition when the homesteaders arrived. More of their ranch later.

When our little town of Mildred came into being in 1908 some of the cowhands I have mentioned decided to give the newcomers a demonstration of the Wild and Wooly West so they dashed into town, fired a few shots and one or two rode their horses into the saloon. The poor bartender had probably heard some of the wild stories that were told to everybody else getting ready to move west and he took off for someplace other than his place of business. When the boys realized that they had actually scared someone, they quietly had their few drinks, pinned a twenty dollar bill to the bar with a horseshoe nail and apologetically crept out of town. Mildred can probably claim the distinction of being the last town 'shot up' by a bunch of cowpunchers. It was about the same as our present day dude-ranch stage being held up by road agents. Just a nostalgic backward look, and all in fun.

I have always wondered where the glamour of cowboy life actually came from. It was really about as glamorous as ditch digging and about equally renumerative. Maybe the Civil War had taught people that the common hand was important. Anyway, there had been a regular blizzard of paperback dime novel fiction about the West; Charlie Russel had been able to picture the common hand in dramatic situations, using the men he knew as models so that they could recognize themselves. Whatever the answer, every kid wanted to be a cowboy.

The real cowboys gradually faded into the scenery, some with ranches and families, some with other jobs in other localities. The last one of these men I saw was in about 1940; he was herding sheep north of Miles City on some of the range where he had gathered cattle some forty years before. At a quarter mile distance, walking along behind sheep and leading his horse he was still unmistakable. To stop would have called back too many memories.

LEARNING TO RIDE RODEO

The three of us boys began learning to ride as soon as opportunity offered. The horses we had were gentle, so offered no excitement, but riding calves was another matter, and the better you became, the bigger steer you tackled. The hide of a steer is much more loose than that of a horse and he has a way of twisting his hind feet one way and his front feet the other. You cinch a rope tight around his middle just behind the front legs, get a good grip on the rope with one hand, kick your feet way ahead and tell the boys to turn him loose.

The riding of cattle is much frowned upon by the owner, as it doesn't help the beef production a bit, and my first share in the riding project was to act as lookout and give due warning when our parents were coming home from town. This went along with good progress for some time but the day came when Mother and Dad went to Terry and were going to be gone for two whole days. About the time there came a slack period in our daily chores, a fair-sized bunch of the neighbor's cattle came to our spring to water. Here was the time, the opportunity, a varied choice of mounts and plenty of them; beside that, we thought the neighbor's cattle should learn to stay at home.

There was no need for a lookout this day as our parents wouldn't be home until the following evening, so we rode steers with varying success most of the afternoon; now, when you get thrown, the thing to do is to let yourself go and fall in the clear; this I failed to do and went under my mount. He stepped on my head and his foot slid off my left eye, taking the hide of my eyelid with it. When I got to the water trough and dunked my head to get the blood and cow manure out of my eye and could still see daylight by holding my eyelids apart we were all much relieved. I still had an eye, but by evening of the next day when the folks got home, it was a thing to behold. That was the end of our homework in the rodeo business. Both Harold and Raymond went on somehow to become good riders; they were older and probably had neighbor friends whose parents were gone at times, but my riding career was somewhat stunted. I have both feet, an arm, a collarbone and a couple of ribs that remind me at times of those days but they were the result of the ordinary run-of-the-mill ranch work. Nothing to complain about as they didn't all happen at once. If you could still walk, you weren't really hurt. You might be 'bugered up a bit' in spots but you weren't really hurt.

Other kids all over the area were going through about the same sort of performances, but the ones at Ismay had about the best condition; there were enough kids to crave excitement, hardly enough to make up a baseball team, there was the town stockyard, and there was range stock handy without the owner's close supervision. Some of them began to get really good at riding anything they could get into the stockyard, and that was

The family of
Percy Wollaston, Sr.,
in front of their
Fairfield, Minnesota, home.

One of the Amundson
women with unidentified
men in front of an early
homestead.

Ned Wollaston's
"proved up" claim
to his homestead.

The Renn homestead,
neighbors to the
Amundsons.

This is presumed to be the Wollaston homestead in the years following its abandonment. Written on the back is "How would you like to live here?"

Myrtle, Percy, and Dean.

Ismay's banker.

The business block,
including the bank,
of Ismay, Montana.

Mrs. Englebritson and
her spotted calf.

Percy Wollaston in
Thompson Falls.

The Wollaston barn,
moved to the Brown
homestead in later years.

the Sunday pastime when the kids from the outlying little ranches could get into town.

Some of the Ismay boys got to the point where they could handle a bronc outside the yards by snubbing him to another saddlehorse and from this they progressed to bucking out a horse or two at picnics and ball games. It always made a welcome diversion and somebody always passed the hat to pay them something for the show. They were a few years older than I, but they came to our little community ball games and picnics so I gradually got to know them.

The two most outstanding riders were Bob Askins and Paddy Ryan. The Askins family had a small ranch out of Ismay and Paddy's mother ran the millinery shop. Altogether our little area was to furnish four world champion rodeo riders, but of course that was a long way into the future. Bob Askins, Paddy Ryan, Howard Tegland from Ismay and Owen Crosby from west of Mildred were all to make the top. Owen was a bareback riding champ and Howard Tegland won his bronc title riding with a broken ankle.

Other people may have been able to ride as tough bucking horses as Bob, but I never saw anyone do as pretty a job of it. These exhibition rides hadn't gone on very long until Bill Roberts, the former XIT man who ran the livery stable in Ismay began to take notice. He had seen a lot of riding in his time and it didn't take him long to recognize talent.

Rodeos at that time were just getting started and there were not many of them but there was one at Belle Fourche and Mr. Roberts took Bob Askins there to enter as a contestant. Bob won the first prize which was a large stuffed mountain lion and as he had no place to keep this trophy at home it was left on display in Roberts' livery barn saddleroom.

After a year or two of standing around in the way in the small saddleroom, the lion's tail got broken and the whole beast was upended and leaned against the wall, more or less forgotten. A friend of mine went into the saddleroom late one night to get his saddle and had some trouble finding it in the dark. You don't go lighting matches in barns unless it's really necessary, but after stumbling around for some time he struck a light and just as he did so he tripped against the mounting board of Bob's old lion. The light flared up just as the snarling face of the toppling trophy got nicely in front of Jack's face. He said that for the instant before he remembered what it was, he was about to go straight through the outside wall.

When the war came on, a lot of the boys enlisted in a group, hoping, I suppose, to be together in one outfit. They went to Miles City, enlisted and started to celebrate. During the evening, somebody shouted out the news that they were out to whip the Germans and some young fellow replied that he was German and proud of it. Paddy Ryan, an innocent-looking diminutive redhead, told him to come on and he would give him something to be proud of. Well, the war started right there, and when the police found what it was all about they simply formed a ring to keep the bystanders back and to see fair play; when the fight was over they took the German to the hospital and little Paddy went on about his celebrating.

After the war, the rodeos became a big business and of course all the good riders gathered at the Miles City rodeo.

During the parade at one of these affairs, Owen Crosby, the bareback champ, was riding along the street roping some of the girls as he went by. The girls were having the thrill of their lives, being roped by a Real Cowboy but some young policeman set himself up to be their protector and suddenly found himself roped and snubbed to a lamp post. The other, older police had a good laugh at his expense and no harm was done except a deflated ego; it was all meant in a spirit of good fun but it was probably just such a bit of tomfoolery that got Owen killed by a Chicago policeman a couple of years later.

There has been too much written already about rodeos and the glamour of cowboying, but these are just the little incidentals that are long forgotten unless one gets to reminiscing.

SIDEBOARDS

Just recently I noticed a little squib in the paper about "Who remembers the old sideboard?" Not many but the antique dealer, surely, but in its time it held an integral part in our culture. I have often thought that surrealist painters were the unimaginative descendants of generations of sideboard carvers, for here the carver of oak really let his fancy run wild. Griffons, acanthus leaves and all sorts of weird creatures were to be seen on sideboards and the more ornate the carving, the greater its dust-catching propensities.

Once installed against the dining room wall, the sideboard was there to stay, furnishing room for all the dishes that any normal family could ever hope to accumulate. There were drawers for silverware and linens, shelves to hold the kerosene lamp and a large mirror to reflect the light therefrom. Here was the hiding place for the nightmare creatures of children's dreams. Here in its uppermost regions were to be found the bottle of strychnine for coyotes, the carbolic acid for disinfectant and the universal cure-all of epsom salts. If you found a rare enough treasure, you might be allowed to keep it in the sideboard, like donating some artifact to the Smithsonian.

Our sideboard was balanced by the cakebox and the decanter, both always nearly full; how the cakebox stayed that way with three growing boys, I'll never know, but the decanter was for medicinal and toasting purposes only. The threat of pneumonia might call for a hot toddy and mustard plaster but we were all as healthy as billygoats. Homesteading in Eastern Montana never furnished cause for toasts or celebration and the thin hairline on the glass marked the slow process of evaporation.

Our old sideboard became the basis of a little family joke when my Aunt Carrie announced that she was coming to visit. She was a housekeeping fanatic of the Nth degree and her furniture glistened from its daily waxing so Mother naturally did a bit of extra housecleaning in anticipation of the visit. Aunt Carrie was a vital, talkative little budget and for the first few days was content to just visit but soon her pent up energy had to have some release, so she suggested housecleaning; Mother agreed and they set about the job but didn't hit much paydirt. When they got to the sideboard, Aunt Carrie just knew that there would surely be a treasure trove of dust behind it. Moving a sideboard was like moving a barn but the two of them dragged it out from the wall. No dust, no cobwebs—nothing. It took all the spice out of Aunt Carrie's visit.

THE WAR AND THE DRY YEARS

When the war came, nobody was prepared for it; yes, of course the generals and the military experts had made all sorts of elaborate plans and told themselves that their strategy was invincible, but nobody, even the Germans, was prepared for the capabilities of technology which were just starting to develop.

Some time in the summer of 1914 a large commercial German submarine appeared at New York, loaded with a cargo of dyes and other fine goods that only German technology was able to produce; it was a promotional stunt for their industries and an overt threat of what they could do, and a sort of chill ran through everybody's mind that a submarine of that size could just pop up out of the sea without warning, but still no one fully realized the threat.

Germany was unprepared for the capabilities of the machine gun in the hands of determined fighters. Belgium, which the whole world could well have expected to stand aside and let the German war machine pass without opposition, decided to fight. We read with disbelief of the windrows and heaps of dead mowed down in those first parade-ground attacks. Belgium held on for two weeks, giving other countries some little time to get organized and those two weeks were the inspiration for millions of scared people.

HOMESTEADING

For most of us, the concept of a nation's size was measured by its news coverage. The idea that Germany was about the size of Montana just didn't occur to us. It seemed that it must be as big as the whole United States. The world we had known had fallen apart, but we couldn't imagine that the war would ever affect us so far away or that it could last very long. Such an insane affair just couldn't last very long.

1915 was a wet year; the wettest we were to see in the sixteen years that I lived there. The crops grew and we had hay to cut and watermelons grew in the garden. Our neighbors, the Dockens, raised some delicious banana squash. They gave us some and we saved the seed for next year, but the next year's squashes were a mixture of all sorts.

More and more people had been moving in, plowing up the land and planting crops. First the steam tractor and later the gasoline ones were used for breaking the larger tracts and it became necessary for us to lease land for grazing and hay land. We also had to plow up more of our land to raise feed.

Water ran in the coulees and the heavier rains washed little gullies in the fields, but there was rain and things would grow almost anywhere as long as there was plenty of moisture.

This was the land of opportunity. Some of the early ranchers had come into the country with nothing but the shirt on their back and wound up owning big ranches. If some had been successful here, others could too, only it would be done by stable farming this time and not the risky type of ranching where a bad winter could wipe out a whole herd.

We now had corrals and feedracks for the stock, a long cattle shed stretched out from the end of the first log cowbarn.

THE WAR AND THE DRY YEARS

Two granaries had been built with a driveway between them and this space roofed over to form an open-ended buggy shed. An icehouse had been built and sawdust hauled from where the sawmill had been to insulate the double walls and to pack the ice. At first we sawed the ice by hand, using the long, coarse-toothed saw that was made especially for sawing ice, but later the Docken boys rigged a circular saw on a small wooden sled, powered by a gasoline engine.

1916 wasn't a very good year, as I remember it. At least I had gotten old enough to ride bogholes by that time. This means riding along the creeks or watering places checking for any stock that might be bogged in the mud. This is only required in spring when some of the cattle are weak and the mud is deeper around the pools. This spring seemed to be unusually bad or there seemed to be more and deeper mud. Somehow the connection between eroded fields and silted waterholes still didn't seem to have registered very much with anybody. The old ranchers had warned against plowing up the range but their advice was long forgotten.

I was pulling one animal out of the mud when my saddle cinch broke. Saddle and I went sailing over the horse's rump and the horse lunged forward to his knees. At times the animal would be too weak to regain its feet after being pulled out and would have to be helped, "tailed up". About the time the old cow got on her feet, she would be mad at the world and whoever had tailed her up had better get to his horse. One of the times when I ran for the horse, he ran too, leaving me with an irate cow. During the work of getting the cow on her feet, I had taken off my jacket, and, after a couple of rounds of footwork, managed to get the jacket flipped over her horns: This occupied the cow long enough for me to get out of close range and to catch my horse.

The summers seemed to get drier and the winters colder as time went on. One winter night our thermometer registered sixty-three degrees below zero. That wasn't just a faulty thermometer, as Dad had gotten a good one which registered maximum and minimum temperatures and used to compare notes with Leon Clark who ran the store and kept weather records. Dad kept some sort of combined ledger, account book and weather record which would be an interesting record now, but like most such things it is long since gone.

As the dry years came on, the most threatening clouds would build up, promising utter deluges of rain. Lightning would flash and the thunder rumble but nothing happened and the storm, if any, seemed to follow the course of Powder River or Fallon Creek. Many is the night I can remember Dad and Mother sitting hopefully and finally despairingly watching the course of these storms.

Some of the storms we did have were stem winders. It was common practice when you unhitched from a hayrack to block the wheel by putting the neckyoke through the spoke so that the wagon couldn't roll away before the wind until it tipped over. As soon as a section of haystack was topped off, it was tied down by baling twine weighted with stones. We were fortunate enough not to be in a hail belt, although we did have a few hail storms. A neighbor's house about five miles away was blown down and the old couple almost beaten to death by hail. They were blown into some little protection but were still beaten black and blue. The grass was beaten out of the ground almost as though the land had been diced.

Lightning storms killed quite a few stock but I don't remember that anyone was killed or any houses struck. I remember one cow that was killed and when the bones were exposed the leg bones were split lengthwise. The current had split them as it sometimes does a tree.

A couple of times we took to the root cellar for shelter, expecting the house to be blown away, but it always stood firm.

PRAIRIE FIRE

The story of the Amundson family covers almost a hundred years of pioneering and I deeply regret not having made some better record of Mrs. Amundson's account.

John Amundson was born in Helgoland, the northernmost part of Norway. Christie Dalager was born in south central Norway, near Christiania, I believe. Her mother died when Christie was about three years old and she lived for some years with her grandparents. Mr. Dalager later remarried and moved to Minnesota along with some other relatives, including an uncle of Christie's. One brother disappeared in the Civil War, probably one of the hundreds killed in action and unrecorded.

When the Dalager menfolks were established in this country, the families were sent for and the story of a pioneering family begins.

John Amundson and Christie Dalager came from Norway on the same ship, were settled as children of families in Minnesota in the same community and later moved with their families to the same community in Dakota, near the town of present day Webster before ever becoming acquainted and later marrying.

Christie was about eight or twelve when she came to America with an aunt, five children and the aunt's mother. The trip took about five weeks at sea and during this short time she learned enough of the English language to get along quite well. The passengers must have supplied some of their own food or perhaps just what they considered delicacies for she mentioned that they all ate at a long table in the central part of the ship while their rooms were along the sides. One day after their meal she remained playing in this dining area after all the others had left except one old fellow who had brought along a small cask of sour milk. As the old man started to pour himself a last swig from his cask, the ship rolled and the cask went gurgling its contents from one side of the dining room to the other. As soon as he caught and stoppered his treat, the old man made himself scarce. Christie said "When the stewards came in, I couldn't understand what they were saying, of course, but they were looking and scolding, I was sure, and wondering what had happened."

Some time during the four or five years in Minnesota, I believe, the aunt lost her husband. Whatever the circumstances, the family set out for Dakota and young Christie, about fifteen or sixteen at the time, walked the entire distance, driving the cows along behind the wagon. They traded milk to Indians along the way for vegetables and once as they stopped to look at an Indian tree burial, an Indian appeared and shook his fist at them to indicate that they were not to molest the grave.

The grass was so tall and lush that the cows had to be milked twice a day in spite of the traveling. Later, on the place where they settled, they twisted grass into tight bundles for fuel and it was this same tall grass which brought tragedy the following year.

We think now of a prairie fire as a not too serious affair because the grass is so short that one can usually step over the flame with no trouble. A fire in those times must have been a different matter entirely.

When they saw the fire coming, the women got the children to a small field they had plowed and went back to the barn to get out the oxen. They were trapped. The grandmother and the oxen were so completely consumed that only one or two small fragments of bone were found. There is a historical marker near Webster today, listing her as the first white woman buried in Dakota Territory. The aunt, being more agile, managed to reach a well and jump into it. Although terribly burned, she survived but was badly crippled for life from the effects of the burns and standing in the icy water for hours before help could be brought to get her out. In spite of this handicap, she raised her family, managed her farm and at her death left considerable property. Young Christie Dalager was living with this aunt and mother at the time and I am not sure when her father remarried, but she later went to live with her father and the new wife.

THE INFLUENZA EPIDEMIC

Christie later met and married the John Amundson who had come over on the same boat, and whose pioneer life had so closely paralleled hers through the years. They were to have eight children, spending most of their married life in Dakota until moving to Montana about 1911.

Mrs. Amundson had a most remarkable career as midwife and nurse for all the illnesses in her community. She had been taken along as help for a midwife first when she was 12 and seemed to have some special talent as a nurse. She must have delivered more than two thousand babies in her lifetime and never lost a patient. She cared for people with smallpox, diphtheria, spotted fever and all the common ailments of children without the slightest concern for her own safety and seemed to be completely immune to everything.

The early years in Dakota must have been hard times beyond anything that we can visualize nowadays. As a girl and young woman, Mrs. Amundson trapped muskrats to obtain a little spending money; the skins sold for around five cents apiece. Many families ate the muskrats themselves. Mr. Amundson once took a load of hay to town in hopes to sell or trade it for cash or groceries, but finally sold it to the store-keeper for twenty-five cents.

Probably the best and most vivid description of the early Dakota days is given by Ole Rolvaag in his "Giants of the Earth." Same locale, same people and same times.

I think there were eight children in the Amundson family, two dying at an early age. As the boys grew older, they began helping at the farm of the crippled aunt who had been burned in the prairie fire years ago. One of the boys, Sufus, mentioned driving the team for her to deliver grain when he was about eight years old. He described a strange happening that occurred one night as he was bringing the team and wagon home long after dark. There was a shower of meteoritic cinders or some sparkling, glowing particles that fell, bouncing off the horse's backs and on the road but without seeming to be hot or heavy enough to affect the animals. He described it as "Looking like they were being poured from a funnel" and lighting up the area near them.

The family began working during the harvest season for a Mr. Frank Buckley, of Ellendale, North Dakota, who had a threshing outfit. Mr. Amundson hauled coal and water for the steam engine and Mrs. Amundson, with the oldest daughter, Almena, did the cooking for the crew in a travelling cook wagon.

The association with the Buckley family lasted throughout the lifetimes of nearly all concerned. The Buckleys moved to Montana in 1897 and started a ranch on upper Cabin Creek, later homesteading at another location in 1908.

Sometime about 1906, Sofus Amundson came to Montana with Buckley, later working as a cowboy for the Paul Renn ranch and homesteading a place of his own about 1908. Later, when the Buckley girls were going to high school in Fallon and 'batching' in a small house, Almena spent one winter with them to attend school.

Nels Amundson, a brother of Sofus, came to Montana and homesteaded on Cabin Creek not far from Sofus' claim and a cousin, who had come to obtain work, was drowned trying to cross the creek during high water. Two other brothers, George and Almer, spent most of their time in Dakota at the home place or working at various jobs until the family moved to Montana in about 1912 and made their home at Sofus' claim.

The boys were capable mechanics, blacksmiths and all around good workmen and soon acquired a well drill which they used to drill the wells on their own places and for many of their neighbors, several of whom never paid even a small part of the expense.

With the coming of war, both Sofus and George went into service. Nels, being married and having a family, was exempt and Almer, the youngest brother, stayed at home to help maintain the farm.

George went through the battles of Chateau Thierry, Argonne Forest and Belleau Woods with no injury other than a badly maimed hand received in an accident on the firing range during training; the cocking piece of his rifle broke and on reporting this to the officer in charge, he was ordered to unload the rifle. As the bolt was released, the rifle fired, driving the bolt back through his hand between his thumb and index finger.

Sofus contracted influenza before finishing training and was evidently regarded as dead for a time. Conditions were so bad that any vacant space in the hospital wards was immediately taken up by new patients, so that he had been wheeled out to some sort of back porch in the cold, probably for the crew who took care of the dead. Whatever the circumstance, he aroused to hear someone say "This man isn't dead" and he was wheeled back into the ward and started on the road to recovery.

No description, however vivid, can give anyone a full realization of what the influenza epidemic was like. Of course there were no antibiotics then or any other medicine which seemed to do any good. Doctors and nurses worked day and night until sheer exhaustion felled them if they were spared from the disease. Coffins or even shipment of the bodies home from the camps were unavailable for long periods.

THE INFLUENZA EPIDEMIC

The flu epidemic didn't strike our part of the country until the following year; in fact, we were not really aware of just how serious it was. The first victim in our own close area was a Mr. Hickman who died in September of what we considered pneumonia and we more or less wondered how he had contracted it in mild fall weather. He died very quickly and we heard little about any other illness until somewhere about the first of November. More and more people became ill and then the schools were closed because of the rapid spread of the disease. People began wearing masks soaked with disinfectant when they attended gatherings or were in crowds but it soon seemed that the ones who took the most precaution were the ones more likely to be stricken.

Leon Clark, the storekeeper, went everywhere, taking medicine or groceries to those who were bedridden and maintained that his ever-present cigar was infallible insurance against illness. This tongue-in-cheek attitude, together with liberal shots of whiskey carried him through the epidemic, going without sleep or rest, carrying hopeless accounts, acting as doctor and arranging funerals. Like so many others, he calmly faced what had to be done and went about it wholeheartedly.

My brother Raymond noticed that his nearest neighbor hadn't started his fires one morning, so went to check whether the family was all right; all of them, six, if I remember rightly were bedridden. One was dead and another child died the next day. That was how quickly the disease could strike and how devastating it could be. Each neighbor looked first thing in the morning to see whether there was a chimney not smoking, for a neighbor might have been hale and hearty one day and unable to get out of bed the next.

Sofus Amundson had returned from the service and, having recovered from the flu, was immune and able to care for his own family when the epidemic reached our district. The death of his oldest sister and of Nel's wife had added four young children to the family and now nearly all of them were taken ill except Sofus and his mother. Together they cared for the sick, cooked and fed stock for themselves and, at one time, nine of the neighbors. Neighbors in those days weren't always just next door, so we can only vaguely imagine the long weary days they must have put in.

All of the family recovered at the time but Mr. Amundson was left in ill health and passed away the following year. This left Sofus as head of a large family and he turned away from a prospective marriage to shoulder the responsibility. From then on until his death many years later he was the good friend of all his neighbors, always ready with a cheerful word or a helping hand to all who knew him.

What rare people most of those first settlers were! Perhaps the isolation and the sheer lack of necessities had something to do with it, for the ones who had the hardest times or had gone through a previous era of pioneer settlement always seemed to be the most cheerful and ready to help at all times.

MOTHER BUCKLEY

The Buckley family moved into Montana from Ellendale, North Dakota where they had farmed and operated a threshing machine in the harvest seasons. I think Mr. Buckley first walked into Montana with two companions, a Mr. Titus and a Mr. Johnson in order to find suitable locations.

For all except cowboys, walking was the old reliable way of getting places in those days and a man could cover a lot of ground in a day. This group located places on upper Cabin Creek and both Buckley and Titus built up fairly profitable horse and cattle ranches.

Mrs. Buckley and their three young daughters came to Montana as soon as the home was established and they operated this ranch until about 1900, when they squatted on land farther down Cabin Creek, building up a ranch there. It was on this ranch that a son was born. Mark Buckley and I later attended high school together, batching for the four years, and he was like a brother to me.

Mr. Buckley had intended to homestead the land where they had started their ranch but a man who had been working for them jumped the claim as soon as homesteading opened hoping to grab an established ranch. So Buckley homesteaded the adjoining land in 1908 and moved the ranch buildings there; it was at this ranch that we later came to know the family and their home was a meeting place for all travelers going through the area.

Mrs. Buckley became Mother Buckley to all the XIT cowboys; the ranch was their home whenever they came that way or needed a job, and she, like her friend Mrs. Amundson, was nurse to every sick neighbor and delivered many a baby.

One of the visitors to the ranch of 1900-1908 was a cattle rustler who I believe was named Jimmy McPete; he and his companions had a hideout dugout near a good spring about five miles from the ranch and from a hill above the dugout, a watchman could see any approaching rider for miles. There was no way to get near the place in daylight without being seen.

These fellows preyed only on the XIT or Krugg ranches which they felt were big enough to be fair game. To any of the smaller ranches or what they considered local ownership they were the best of neighbors, minding their own business or lending help at branding time.

McPete carried a beatup looking old six-shooter that had some gunnysacking wrapped around its broken grips but he was regarded as being very handy with it. A sheriff and deputy surprised him and a companion just as they were getting on their horses to leave Fallon one day. The friend, who wasn't wanted, made some move to distract the officers' attention for a fraction of a second and they found themselves confronted with this same beat up old gun. McPete had trained his horse to walk sideways and he kept the officers covered until he was out of range for any ordinary shot, then whirled and got out of there. By the time a posse was organized he was well beyond chance of being overtaken.

I heard that in about 1916 or '18 he had married and settled down to an ordinary quiet life on a small ranch somewhere near Billings, but some officers recognized him; one day when he appeared in town, they went to the ranch, hid in the barn and waited for him. He was killed while resisting arrest when he came home.

The Buckleys owned the land where the old hideout had been at the time Mark and I were going to high school, but the old dugout was still visible; hidden in the bottom of a coulee, with a ditch dug around it to deflect any water from runoff in spring or during a rain, it would have been unnoticed by anyone only a few yards away. What a fine view from their lookout hill! Miles of rolling hills and prairie to where the Fallon Flats dropped off to the Yellowstone River.

The three Buckley girls grew up as nieces to a crew of doting uncles, the XIT cowboys who came visiting Mr. and Mrs. Buckley and taught the girls to ride and rope with the best cowhands. When the time came for them to attend high school, they and Mrs. Buckley rented a small house in Fallon. It was there that their friend Almena Amundson stayed to go to school.

Mr. Buckley was a very well-read man, interested in politics or community affairs and became the first representative for Prairie County when it was formed in 1915.

THE PET MONKEY

Even the most astute of men are entitled to a lapse of judgment where their children are concerned and the devil must have laughed outright when Frank Buckley returned from one of his trips back to Dakota bringing a pet monkey for his young daughters.

I have asked one or two of the old-timers who remember this beast what they could tell me about him; a strange you-wouldn't-believe-me-anyway look would come over their faces, but from the best I could gather, he must have covered a range of about thirty miles long by fifteen or twenty wide.

I base this estimate on reports of his appearances and the distance that a stampeding steer could run, because he had no sooner witnessed a couple of bronc riding exhibitions than he could vie with the best of rodeo riders. Here was a sport right down his alley. He quickly learned that horses were alert and could kick dangerously, but that steers were available almost everywhere and had a handy tail to catch hold of. Pulling the feathers out of chickens was all right when there was nothing better to do to go for a center across the prairie on the back of a bawling terror stricken steer was just the thing he could really enjoy. He would go flicking through the sagebrush like a shadow, catch an unsuspecting steer by the tail, land on its back and nothing but sheer boredom or interest in some other mischief could dislodge him. The steer would run until exhausted and when his passenger decided to go home he caught himself another mount that was pointed in the right direction. This was to finally be his undoing, but he made things lively for a long time; much longer than his neighbor victims would have liked.

At that time, houses were never locked and if no one was home, the hungry traveller was welcome to fix himself a meal. Now here was a traveller who was nearly always hungry, ravenous, in fact, and who not only found himself a meal but stuffed the pouches of his cheeks to take along for a snack. He relished dried fruit, especially dried prunes, and was able to find them no matter how well hidden. He was not maliciously destructive, but would upset things in his search and didn't bother to tidy up either.

One irate wolfer, whose camp had been raided, set a pack of five wolfhounds after him; he whipped the entire pack handily although they had never backed down for a wolf. He would light on a hound's back, a screeching all of fury and when the dog rolled, he was gone to the next customer. Nobody wanted to shoot him and rather admired him in a way, but would have loved to outwit him in some way.

One fellow set out coyote traps baited with prunes. The monkey had never seen traps but sat down to study the whole thing over carefully; after a while he hunted up a stick with which he turned the traps over and sprung them, then racked out the prunes. The same procedure with another who tried to catch him in a box trap.

While one of the XIT boys was visiting Buckleys and having coffee they heard his horse squealing and trying to tear the barn down. There was the monkey, quirting and kicking the horse in full rodeo style and the horse nearly in hysterics. All these little capers didn't gain him much popularity but people soon began to expect him almost anyplace.

Charlie Mackay, who had a ranch on Fallon Creek, a good twenty miles or more from Buckley's ranch, set out for town one day with another rancher, a Frenchman, to get supplies. After their shopping the Frenchman took on quite a few too many drinks, so on the long drowsy ride home he dozed off for a nap; when he awakened he stretched, looked around to see where they were and suddenly stiffened up saying "Charlie, you see something back there?" When Mackay looked back he saw Buckley's net stuffing his cheeks with some dried fruit they had bought with their other groceries. Now here was a chance too good to miss and Charlie kept a straight face while saying he didn't see anything wrong. After a number of surreptitious looks back, the Frenchman turned again. "Charlie, you sure you don't see nothing?"

About that time Mr. Monkey went flitting off into the sagebrush and Charlie could truthfully swear he couldn't see a thing.

The three Buckley girls used to take turn-about in doing the housework. Their efficient German mother saw to a rigid training in cooking, cleaning, gardening and all the rest as well as becoming top cowhands; she also made sure there were always the best magazines and literature about the house and that the girls read them; for example, in doing the supper dishes, one girl washed, one dried, and the third was free to study, sew or read.

One evening as the supper dishes were being washed up, May, who had the free evening and was reading and sunk deep in one of the big old leather chairs, could also have a view of part of the kitchen; she could see "Monkee" who had finished his supper and was relaxing on his private shelf, high on the kitchen wall. He was meditatively picking his teeth as he had so often seen the cowhands do after their supper, gazing vacantly into space and completely at ease.

As the girls finished the dishes, the one who was drying put some pot covers and frying pan lids in a rack which hung beside the stove, spread the dishtowel neatly on its rack to dry and both retired to the living room. They had no sooner disappeared than Monkee was down like lightning, snatched the pan lids from their rack, redried and replaced them, put the dishtowel back as neatly as ever and was back on his shelf as the very picture of innocence.

The end came late one fall when the family set off for a trip to Fallon; that was a drive of some twenty miles and that much of a buggy ride can be a boring affair for even the most sedate of passengers. The monkey endured the trip without complaint most of the way but finally they passed a herd of cattle grazing; this was just too much to bear and he was gone, streaking through the sagebrush, snatching a steer's tail, onto his back and away went the whole herd at full speed.

The following spring one of the hands on the roundup found a little pile of bones huddled under a sagebrush. An early storm had caught another pioneer.

THE BANK

When the businessmen at Mildred decided to start a bank they brought in an easy-going, sandy haired Missourian as manager. At the end of the first month everybody in the area knew Hayden Bright and he knew their first names, the names and ages of their children and the potential of every farm and its operator.

Hayden, he wasn't Mr. Bright, even to the kids, used to drive a Ford touring car with the top down and usually with its gas lever to the bottom of its arc. He had a brindle bulldog which was the most compact bundle of muscle and energy I have ever seen. They would start out from the bank to visit some farm or ranch and the dog rode happily beside him only until they saw the first jackrabbit, then would go sailing out of the car, roll like a ball for a couple of yards and come up at full speed. A jackrabbit cannot run much more than a mile at full speed and that dog could have run two of them into the ground as far as endurance was concerned but he soon lost sight of the rabbit and set out to catch up with the car. The roads followed the section lines then and the dog would cut across the land, always seeming to sense where his master would go. I always enjoyed seeing Hayden and his dog going anywhere. Top speed was cruising for both of them but the car did have to slow down somewhat for corners and the dog would either catch up or they would arrive at their destination. Both man and dog could appear utterly relaxed when not going anywhere, both were the most amiable and friendly of personalities and like his master, the dog seemed to know everybody and like them.

When the war came on, each bank was allotted some amount of liberty bonds proportional to the population or maybe prosperity of their territory. They were supposed to see to the selling of these bonds and they set about it pretty willingly because the bonds only paid somewhere around three and one-half percent, while the banks were charging ten; here is how the deal worked; you were stone broke for cash usually, but if you didn't buy at least one hundred dollar bond you were a slacker and believe me that was a bad word in those times when sauerkraut was liberty cabbage and every draft dodger was wearing military cut clothes.

When you were both patriotic and broke, you went to the bank and borrowed the money. They loaned you the hundred dollars at ten percent, held the bond as security, and, after the war was over and you wanted to sell the damned thing, they bought it from you for eighty dollars. That was a pretty good plum for the banking industry as far as the ordinary fellow could see it and it stayed in memory for a long time. That, and some of the abscondings and failures that came a little later when the war boom was over, gave banks a bad name they didn't deserve generally.

There weren't as many strict rules controlling the banks then as there are now and no such idea as deposit insurance. You depended on the integrity of the banker and he depended on yours. There were probably almost as many crooks and incompetents among bankers as there are among preachers, but they got to handle a lot more of your money. Some didn't live up to trust, true enough, but the majority were doing their best to help their community grow and prosper. If they made a dime while helping you to make a nickel, more power to them and I will try to show some of the human side of the banker. In order to do so, I'll carry on a little history of my brother Raymond's dealings with Hayden Bright.

Ray had set out on his own by this time, leasing a place and putting in a small crop; he had worked and saved and traded until he had some horses, a little machinery, and with his last spare cash he had bought a shiny new top buggy to go courting a girl who was to be the highlight of his life for more than fifty years.

When the time came to get married, Ray was flat broke, flat, stony broke in a way people wouldn't understand nowadays; sure, he had a crop going, owned some equipment and a good saddlehorse and his credit was good for groceries at the store, and he had a small crop loan with Hayden at the bank, but as for cold cash he didn't have two dimes to rub together.

HOMESTEADING

You didn't go back to the bank and ask for an extension on your loan unless there was some really drastic circumstance and just getting married didn't count that way.

I happened to have hoarded my trapping and coyote bounty money to the whole sum of $27.50 which I loaned him. Our good neighbor, Art Docken, took them to Terry in his new Dodge car and the wedding went off in style.

So the new bride and groom settled down to life on a dry land farm, as blissfully happy as any young couple ever was. They were so broke that one time when they had to get a sack of flour, they heard the good news that it was fifty cents cheaper per sack in Ismay than in Mildred and, fixing a picnic lunch, they drove some eight miles farther to make the saving. It took an all day drive, but life was new and they were sharing it together.

Hayden had a way of setting up deals to help the bank's customers that made them seem to have just happened accidentally or by the customer's own ideas so when the little farms didn't much more than pay off Ray's loan, it just sort of came up in conversation that there was a farm and cattle ranch a couple of miles east of Mildred that was needing a good manager. The job paid fifty dollars a month in salary plus a share of whatever crop and stock the place produced.

The ranch was owned by a Dr. Thompson, an eye, ear, nose and throat surgeon from Chicago, and his partner, an importer, a Mr. Lawton. They "just happened" to be in town one day when Ray and his wife came in for groceries and just happened to meet, with the result that Ray got the job of managing the place and Dr. Thompson went back to Chicago confident that, barring poor ground and bad weather, the place would show a profit.

THE BANK

The war had brought wheat prices up to almost three dollars a bushel and a lot of farmers were sure the price would go to three or better. Ray had several hundred bushels and decided to sell at the going market. He decided to wait until after lunch before going to town, and see what the prices were for the next day, as the elevators received the price quotations at noon. That was the day the price dropped a dollar a bushel. Such are the fortunes of farming: You may have a good year's profit almost in hand and have it vanish overnight.

One year there was a fair crop but the grain got damp during harvest and began to heat in the bins. In spite of all his efforts to turn and dry the grain, Ray could not get the stuff fit for sale and it began to go from bad to worse; he finally went to the bank to explain what was wrong and why there was a delay on the crop loan payment.

Hayden listened to the explanation and finally said, "Any suggestions?" Ray explained that the only solution he could think of was to get some young pigs and feed the grain to them as they were being readied for market. Hayden shoved a new checkbook over the desk to him and said "Take this and don't come back until you've got some hogs. And when you write out the check, don't act timid; write 'er out as though you had all the money in the world."

Ray located the pigs, seventy-five half starved looking weaners not much bigger than jackrabbits and brought them all home in one load by putting boards between the divisions of a three-box grain wagon.

For the first few days the pigs ate as though there was no limit to their appetite, then they began to enjoy the comfort of clean straw beds and would rest until they thought a light snack would be agreeable. I helped Ray drive them to the stock-yard for shipping when they were ready for market and they were a fine looking lot of porkers, indeed.

Ray and I were reminiscing about old days recently (1974) and neither of us could remember whether he had even signed a note for the loan on these hogs. At any rate, he shipped them to market, collected the pay and went back to Hayden to pay off the loan. The banker knew you as an individual instead of an account number as so often is the case now. He helped more than he legally should, sometimes, perhaps, but he had the good of the community and his customer at heart.

Time ran until Ray had accumulated a cash surplus of $1,900 when one of his brother-in-laws patented some sort of chemical for preventing corrosion on battery terminals. A second brother-in-law, who was a born promoter, undertook to manage the business affairs, and, with Ray's capital, they set off for Minneapolis to get their product on the market. The promoter-manager soon struck up a rosy sounding agreement with some fly-by-night company that was looking for something that would sell without advertising and thereby save themselves from insolvency.

Ray's $1,900 carried him and his wife and the two brothers through most of that winter with the help of a few odd jobs. The cost of living in the city must have been a lot different then than now, because Ray and his wife seem to have had a good time and enjoyed quite a bit of entertainment, but he was broke again and set out to make a fresh start.

The bank in Mildred had closed by this time and Hayden Bright was in a bank at Miles City. When Ray hesitantly went

THE BANK

to the bank, there was Hayden, leaned back lazily in his chair with his feet on the desk. The door of his office was open so that he could see everyone who came in the door, and he called out, "Hello, Ray, come on in." They visited for a few minutes, and then: "So, you lost your money, huh?" Best thing that ever happened to you. Now, how much are you going to need to get started again?"

Ray allowed he thought that he and a friend who had some contracting experience had a chance to get a contract moving dirt for the railroad, tearing out some old fills if they could get an outfit together. Horses could be bought in the Miles City stock sales for eight or ten dollars a head, they could get some second-hand harness and fresnos fairly cheap and be in business.

The deal was made and Ray went out of there ready to tackle the world again. There were many rough times later, of course, but that little friendly gesture and confidence in his ability was a turning point in life for him.

The new venture made a good profit. It was hard, grueling, dusty work, but they were on their way up. They might get a horse that had run the range for five or six years without a rope on him, but once they got him harnessed to three other horses who had pulled fresno for a few days, he soon gave up fighting and decided that plain work was bad enough without struggling. The only real defeat came from a mule which fell off the side of the fill as he was fighting the harness. To get him back in the team he had to be unharnessed, and he was smart enough to collapse every time he got anywhere near the edge of an embankment. He went back to the sales ring with their hope that he went to the glue factory.

HOMESTEADING

Raymond and his wife had rented an apartment in Miles City so one Saturday evening Ray decided to catch the passenger train as it came past their job and ride in to Miles for the weekend.

The trains would go slowly as they passed over the soft part of the fill where they were working, so it should be a simple matter to swing onto the car. One little thing went wrong with the plan, though; when the engineer got his heavy engine safely across the weak spot, he began picking up speed. Ray saw that he would never be able to catch the platform of the last car because the train would be travelling much too fast by then, so he caught hold of one of the steps and swung himself in under the little platform which closes off the steps when the train is in motion. This is the way he rode some seventy miles in the dark and cold, so by the time they pulled into the yards at Miles City he was looking for a quick way to get off.

He heard the porter come onto the platform and open the top half of the doorway and could picture him leaning out the door as they do to see the approaching station. He reached up to grasp the top of the lower half door in order to swing off the step and in doing so put his hand on that of the porter. The poor man was so petrified that he didn't even attempt to move his hand. "Lawd, Lawd, ooooohh Lawd!" he yelled. We've often wondered just what his thoughts were.

THE LOST STEER

The dirt moving job was the last that Ray worked in the area and set him moving around in search of something permanent but I have always thought that his decision to get away from farming and the dryland area entirely started through one of the odd happenstances that we don't take any notice of at the time. It came about this way: While he was still operating the farm and ranch for Dr. Thompson and Mr. Lawton, an old fellow with a camping outfit stopped and asked for water. It was fairly late in the afternoon, so they visited a while, the man asked whether he might camp there for the night and so that was agreed.

I don't remember just what kind of an outfit the old boy had, but it was good equipment for the times and he appeared like someone who had made his stake in business, retired, and set out to go wherever he'd missed going when he was younger and willing to take his time doing it. There weren't the campers and trailers that are so common now: Everybody sort of fixed up their own camping outfit to suit their own ideas. Some had tents, some had a canvas fly that pulled over the side of the car and some had affairs that folded out for both shelter and storage for cooking. It was quite the thing to pull into a campground, show off by setting up your camp in a jiffy and have supper ready before somebody else had even got unpacked.

The old man set up his camp, fixed his meal and strolled around looking the place over. He visited with Ray and helped a little with chores to be sociable, probably sizing up Ray's situation with an accuracy that we had no conception of at that time. Finally he asked just what Ray was trying to do there, what his goal and motive was. Ray replied that he hadn't really thought much about it in that way, except that he was trying to get a start in life and make a little money. The old man said "Always remember, if you want to make money, you have to go to where the money is." The next morning, the old fellow went quietly on his way with a courteous thank you but he had left a lasting impression that paid for his lodging many times in later years.

During the time that Ray was running the ranch, he got word through the stockmen's association that one of his steers had drifted or been driven far off the range by getting mixed in some other herd. The farmer who reported the stray lived some twenty miles to the South of our place, making it about thirty-five from Ray's, so he rode into our place for an overnight stop and visit and I went along with him the next morning.

We left home about five in the morning in the dark and cold, as it was late fall. There was snow on the ground and cold enough that we rode much of the time trying to rattle our feet around in the stirrups to keep from freezing our toes. Along about midday we began getting into the area where we thought we might find the man we were looking for and began to stop at places to inquire. We also sort of hoped for an invitation to a meal or at least a hot cup of coffee. None of the people seemed to know anybody more than two miles from their own yard and should only give the most vague directions about the area beyond that. Some were obviously just getting ready for dinner and later one or two came out picking their teeth. I was a growing kid then and hungry any time within a half hour after the last meal or maybe this was the first time I'd been out beyond the range of our own close acquaintances and suddenly and permanently I despised the whole cheap corncracking lot of them and what they had done to a land where less than ten years earlier any traveler was offered hospitality. I wanted no part of these people or any district where they lived and made up my mind to start looking for some way of getting out.

We finally located the man who had Ray's steer, paid him for reporting the animal and what feed he reckoned we owed although any sign of feed was nonexistent, and then asked if we could buy some sort of meal. The men fried some bread dough and thin steak and fixed some coffee and it still stands out in memory as one of life's best meals, but there was a different texture, flavor and appearance about the stack from any we had ever tried before. After dinner, when we went out to the barnyard to get the steer, we noticed a yearling colt lying frozen in the yard: One hind quarter had been hacked off with an axe after the animal had frozen and we both knew then what kind of steak we had had. Well, we had both been hungry enough so that the steak stayed down, no matter what ailment the colt had died from and we set out for home about an hour before dusk. It was still plenty cold but we certainly weren't hungry just then.

We made good time on the way home. The steer wasn't tired, our horses had had some rest while we were chewing up some relative of theirs, and they wanted to get back to their own stalls. We let them set their own course, out across country as best the fence lines would allow and just before dark we came in sight of a ranch. A regular, old time ranch, with its low, snug looking buildings, its corrals and its haystacks, and there was light in the windows and smoke in the chimneys.

Here was supper and shelter for the night for us and our animals along with an unquestioning hospitality just as surely as those buildings were standing there before us. We weren't sure of our location but knew that the Bowden ranch was somewhere in the area and that was what it proved to be. I am not sure whether either of us had even seen Mr. or Mrs. Bowden before and certainly they were only vaguely aware of our existence at most, but were immediately made as welcome as though they had known us always. Mr. Bowden and Dad were acquainted, of course, and I had seen their two older children, Floyd, the oldest and Joyce, a girl slightly older than I at dances occasionally in the Whitney Creek community hall.

I believe both Mr. and Mrs. Bowden had some Spanish ancestry as he was small, wiry and deeply tanned, while she was a fairly tall, dark and rather regal looking woman. They also had a young son, Robert, a lad of about six, and as bursting a bunch of energy as I've ever seen.

Floyd was not at home that evening, possibly away at college or work somewhere and Joyce had died recently of septicemia, linked by scandal with the then rodeo hero of the day. I remember, and didn't fully understand at the time that Mr. Bowden brought up the subject of her death. He was trying in a heartbroken parent's blind way to reach some sort of understanding with youth as we must have represented it to him, and saying, "She just growed up ahead of her age." Joyce had died, singing in her final delirium the then popular song of whispering. "Darling I have something to tell you. Darling I have something to say."— Poor, scared, lonely little girl, who had just "Growed up ahead of her time."

Misfortune and tragedy seems to have singled out this family for special attention. Mr. Bowden had helped and loaned money to many of the homesteaders around him and seldom been repaid in any way, there had been a case of cattle rustling in which he refused to prosecute and within a year or two after our visit to the ranch, he was killed by a fall from a horse.

On the night after Mr. Bowden's funeral, one of their neighbors was mysteriously shot down as he went to investigate a noise in the barn; the tracks of the killer's horse lead toward the Bowden ranch and a lot of excited neighborhood rumors brought suspicion down upon Floyd. Some of the ones who had been helped by the Bowdens were ready with all manner of surmises and rumor and this must have been a bitter pill to an already griefstricken family. Within another year or two, Mrs. Bowden was found dead on the prairie, partly eaten by coyotes or other animals.

Years later, a construction worker was to leave the job without even stopping to collect his pay when he learned that one of the other workers had known the murdered man and had been in the neighborhood when the murder occurred. He had mentioned to one of the other workers that he had been sent to prison by a man named Oster. Oster was the name of the murdered man. Who knows, after more than fifty years?

MY FIRST GUN

In my gun cabinet is an old rifle which, to me, brings back the whole long chain of our homesteading days; ugly and obsolete as the military thinking which produced it, it has been "sporterized" by trimming down the forepart of the full-length stock which it originally had and cutting off half of the magazine. At the time when I first saw it, it was hanging on the wall of the Docken Brother's bunkhouse and that is where it stayed until about 1920. It had been given to Art Docken by some friend in Minneapolis who had first acquired it from some importing company which sold bargain army surplus equipment. The new owner dressed it up to suit his fancy and went out with some friends to try it out in target practice. During some of this practice, a piece of shattered rock or a spatter of one of the bullet flew back, striking one of the party in the eye end blinding him. Needless to say, that was all the man wanted to see of his new gun, so he destroyed the ammunition and gave the gun to Art as a collection piece. Art had several antiques, including a fine Navaho blanket, so when the brothers came to Montana and built a bunkhouse living quarters in one half of their granary building, one wall of their bunkhouse was decorated with blanket and antique guns. There was also a fine 16 gauge double with a Krupp barrel which my son Dean now has.

The guns stayed in place as decoration, with the exception of the shotgun, until some time after the First World War, when the young men who had come with the Dockens as hired man returned from the service and again took up residence in his old living quarters, the bunkhouse. One winter evening, as chores were being done, the old familiar heating-stove accident happened; the stove was stoked with lignite coal and the damper closed. The gas formed by the smouldering coal finally ignited and blew the damper open, scattering coals on the floor. By the time chores were finished, a fire had started but consumed most of the oxygen in the

MY FIRST GUN

room and was just smouldering but the place was a mess of smoked up walls and ceiling. It was during this housecleaning that Will Docken decided to sell the guns. Art had moved back to Minneapolis and had no further interest in collecting, so Dad bought the shotgun and I bought the old rifle as a collector's piece with no idea that there was any possibility of obtaining ammunition for it.

Not too long after my new acquisition somebody came along with the information that a man had a gun of the same type for sale, together with a box of ammunition. The grass didn't have a chance to get any higher before I had that other rifle and the box of shells. Now I was in business with something that would shoot. The other rifle had been sawed off to carbine length and was even more homely looking than my first one, so I sold it, keeping most of the shells, but I had learned the calibre of the gun, and even found out that Remington still sold such cartridges, so I set about carrying my new rifle, never yet having fired it because I didn't have many cartridges. The chance to shoot finally came when I saw a coyote and I waited until he turned broadside to take a second look. For a second or two a billowing puff of white smoke obscured any forward view and then there was my coyote without even a twitch. I had paid $2.50 for the gun and got $2.65 for the hide. Such was my degree of finance.

I learned that my newly acquired rifle was called a .43 Egyptian; whether the Egyptian government had used them as an official military rifle or not, I have never found out; but my search for ammunition soon led me to one of the instances I mentioned before, that of people being influenced by wild rumor into bringing unnecessary equipment.

HOMESTEADING

I was told that Mr. Ralph Norris, who had a claim east of Mildred had all or some part of a case of this calibre ammunition and promptly set out to see about it.

Mr. Norris had come to Mildred in 1910 and I doubt that he had ever had the least experience in farming before taking up his claim. One of his first experiences came when he started to unhitch his team at first arrival at the claim; he had stopped the wagon on a downhill grade and took down the neckyoke, leaving the wagonwheels unblocked. The wagon rolled ahead starting to crowd the horses and they ran away, upsetting the load of household goods. He had started to learn, the hard way, as so many others had to do.

Mr. Norris was a graduate of the University of Illinois in Chicago and at one time had held the world's record at pole-vaulting. He was a good track man and used to keep in training for several years after coming to Montana. Mrs. Norris had come out in 1912 and taken up adjoining land and becoming his wife. I was always under the impression that she or both of them had come west in hope of regaining her heath, as she suffered from tuberculosis. Both fine, cultured people, but seemingly so ill-suited to life on a claim.

Mr. Norris explained that when they considered coming to Montana, they weren't sure what conditions might be, as they had heard all sorts of wild stories, and thought possibly they might be attacked, so he had bought seven of the rifles and a case of ammunition. The idea seems laughable to us now, but here were two inexperienced young people setting out to face whatever the world had in store for them.

I'll say one thing for the idea; anybody with seven of those rifles and a case of ammunition could have been nothing to take lightly, then or any time since. The big bottle-necked cartridge with its .43 calibre bullet is a collector's item now, worth more than I paid for the rifle itself, but anything that got in the way of one of those slow, lumbering bullets of lead wasn't going to do any more attacking.

THE AGATE RING

Somewhere around the country there is an agate ring whose dendritic inclusion depicts a western type saddle.

The ring was given to a man named Jack Rhody by the people of Mildred as a token of friendship and esteem when he left to enter service during the First World War.

Jack seems to have appeared out of nowhere shortly after the town started and that seems to be as far back as anyone's information about him ever got.

A trimly built, medium-sized man of about 160 pounds, invariably quiet and courteous, polite and friendly to all and yet he might as well have materialized out of thin air as far as background was concerned.

He was reported to be serving as deputy sheriff but never served any summons and nobody wanted to be disorderly around him. The only man I ever heard of tangling with him regained consciousness two and a half days later. He did act as a locator of claims for settlers at times and it was on one of these trips that he and the prospective settler stopped for dinner at the home of our neighbor, Mr. Worsell.

There was a five hundred dollar penalty for shooting antelope at the time but groceries were scarce and Worsell had just got himself some fresh meat. You gave guests the best you had and the new settler kept exclaiming about how delicious the steak was and what kind of meat was it anyway, beef or pork? After two or three of these queries had been turned aside as tactfully and unobtrusively as possible, Jack finally put down his fork and said, mildly, "Well, I'll tell you, it's neither beef nor pork." End of questions.

Jack had yellow eyes like a coyote's and, although I surely wish to be wrong, I always had the impression that the pupils were vertical slits like a cat's. They gave you a chilly feeling.

At that time, women had begun to wear divided riding skirts and ride astride. The oldest of the Buckley girls still had a beautiful side saddle hanging around but by then ranch girls, when they rode, wore the conventional California pants and riding boots of the well dressed cowpuncher. That seemed proper enough: They were slim-hipped, wiry young ladies who seemed no different than any other ranch hand but if the ordinary household female wanted to go riding, she wore a long, voluminous divided skirt, really a pair of pants with grossly overgrown legs. It sometimes took the ordinary horse quite a while to tolerate this flapping contraption. No wonder the horse objected, they looked kind of silly, even in spite of convention and style.

Jack had undertaken to gentle a pretty snuffy bronc to be safe for some lady to ride and in the process had donned one of these skirts. Can you imagine one of our cinema star cowboys riding up the street of his hometown in any such get-up? It was all part of the gentling process and accepted as such, if there was any kidding at all it was done by mighty close friends.

The breaking process was going along just fine when one of the two dogs charged out and nipped the horse's heels. That was just too much for the horse and he unwound in spite of all Jack could do to keep him calm: It undid a lot of patient and embarrassing work and it also undid the town's peace and quiet for a short time, for the horse had no sooner run out of steam than dogs began getting scarce. Woe betide the pooch that wasn't in his own yard and minding his own business. Nine dogs in nine shots confirmed what we and all surmised before: Jack would only stand about so much provocation and he was extremely fast and accurate with a gun.

When he went into the service, his skill with a gun promptly won the state's highest score with machine gun, but then in training for the use of gas masks the men were put in a room or tank filled with gas. Jack's mask proved to be defective and his lungs were damaged. Tuberculosis quickly developed and he was discharged as an invalid. He came home to the little community he had adopted but spent his last few weeks in the hospital at Miles City. When his body was returned for burial, his ring which he had worn so proudly had been stolen. Some corpse robber probably wore that ring, but he wouldn't have worn it long if any of the people around Mildred had recognized it.

SHOTS AT O'FALLON

There has been so much nonsense in television shows, movies and paperback novels about the gunman, badman or whatever you call him that the whole subject has become preposterous.

Sure, there were homicidal maniacs, just as we have them today, but probably less of them, percentage-wise. There were veterans of the Civil War or the rough times that followed shortly after. If some young fellow got into trouble and a shooting followed, there was always some revengeful relative or the mindless boob type who challenges the champion prize fighter.

The very little I have been able to gather through hearsay or from the few old-timers who actually knew any of them, these men were mainly trying to live quietly and stay out of trouble.

There was a shooting at Fallon, or O'Fallon as it was then called, at about the end of the cattle period and accounts of it seem to bear this out: True, the man who did the shooting was recognized as a gunman, but let's consider the story.

One of the beef-shipping crews had delivered their herd and seen it off on the train: They had drawn pay and were having their night on the town before going back to the roundup for another herd. One of the fellows became maudlin, stumbling drunk, and another member of the crew, a colored man, began picking on him and pushing him off his feet. None of the men wanted to interfere because the colored man was in a mean and quarrelsome mood himself, but the gunman, Henry Thompson, finally protested and told him to stop. He continued bothering the drunk until Thompson told him that was enough, and to stop. That ended the persecution of the drunk but the Negro continued drinking and boasted that he was going to kill himself a white man before morning. Morning came and he had obtained a rifle. As he rode up in front of the saloon, Thompson stepped out to face him and he started to draw the rifle. That was the end, of course, but here we see one of these "bad men" trying to pacify brewing trouble, giving the other fellow plenty of opportunity to back away and behave sensibly and at the last, taking a responsibility that nobody else wanted to assume.

You would say "why not call the marshall?" The marshall, if any, was probably some fellow with a family and in need of a job. Leading the ordinary drunk off to jail and giving him a place to sleep it off without doing any harm was his main chore. If he was aware of real trouble, he wisely found business somewhere else and left the matter in more competent hands. I think Thompson was finally killed at Malta, but never heard any details.

Our little town of Mildred was to have had a deputy sheriff acting as peace officer almost from its beginning but I can't remember any serious offenses or disturbances. Perhaps there was a little less law and more prompt enforcement. One fellow got himself arrested for disturbing the peace or causing trouble in some way and after the arrest the deputy was asked "What are you going to do with him? We haven't any jail to put him in." The deputy replied, "Doneed one." He simply handcuffed the prisoner's arms around a hitching post and went to lunch. After two or three hours of standing there in the hot sun and the amused smiles of passers-by the prisoner was turned loose. Neither he or anyone else felt like disturbing the peace for a long time.

Bob Askins, the rodeochamp, got too much to drink one afternoon in Terry and parked his car on the sidewalk. When the town marshall tried to get him to move, he knocked the marshall down and settled for a nap in his car. Now it was up to some higher authority. The deputy sheriff was like the army sergeant; he was the one who really kept things in order and going smoothly. Now, deputy Bill Howard was an old Texas cowhand, quiet and easygoing but when he woke Bob and asked him to back off the sidewalk, Bob still wanted to have trouble: He was a good boxer and fast but when he started to hit, old Bill was faster yet. He had a luger in his shoulder holster and laid it down on top of Bob's head. He tossed Bob into the back seat, gave him a night's lodging in the jail and they parted good friends in the morning. Maybe not just up to legal standards as we know them now, but somehow it worked.

In trying to look back over the years I notice a characteristic of the early homesteaders which seem like the opposite of our present time. Today, when people start getting acquainted, much of their conversation is taken up by descriptions of back home and the conditions there. There seems to be some lack of looking forward as those people did.

There were people from almost every walk of life and status of education, but they learned little of each other beyond what each planned to make of his place and plans for the future of the community. The next meal might be potatoes and water gravy but you didn't hear anything about hardship unless somebody burned out or broke a leg.

The only family that I knew much about was that of my brother-in-law, James J. (Jim) Morrow. Jim had learned the plumber's trade by starting out as an apprentice boy—probably as soon as he was able to do any work at all, as he married early, almost a boy and was a journeyman plumber and a good one at that time. Three children arrived in rapid succession so he began to think of establishing a permanent home. In Minneapolis, where they lived, he had to work for an established plumbing contractor.

When homesteads were available, there was a chance to get land of their own, to have a home of their own, and, surely, where a new community was growing up, there would be plumbing to install, a young couple could start up in business in a small way and grow with the community.

The dreams of all the newcomers must have been similarly rosy and similarly dampened by one circumstance or another. To begin with, nobody had any money beyond the bare minimum. And usually less than that. Nearly all of the plumbing stayed outdoors for the following twenty years. Jim supported his family by contracting jobs along the border of the Dakotas where building was acquiring a more permanent status, but this left his family to manage by themselves at home on the claim most of the time. It was a rough training but produced the most competent and self-sufficient bunch of young citizens I've ever known.

In April of 1908, Mildred must have been about the end of the line for the Milwaukee railroad: That was when Jim arrived and took up his claim about a mile and a half west of the town. He wanted to be near enough to town so that the children could go to school and that he could go to work in case there was a demand for plumbing. The claim he chose contained about fifteen acres of flat tillable land and the remainder consisted of a huge gumbo swale where erosion had eaten its way out from the Fallon Creek channel . . . Jim was a fast and indefatigable worker but I remember him saying that when he arrived and got his freight bill paid he had just fifty cents left. Nobody seemed to have any cash money; they all wanted to exchange work so I don't know how he managed to get enough lumber to build at but he did build a tarpaper two story shelter partially dug back into the hillside.

Digging any sort of footing for a house in damp gumbo by hand is no small job but somehow he got it done and the house frame up and sheeted in.

DIGGING A WELL

I remember Jim Morrow's description of that day when he got the last of the sheeting on his shack and began to put tarpaper on the outside along toward evening. He could laugh about the trouble and hardship when I was old enough to know him but his description of that day and his subsequent letter home to his wife may give you a better idea of the new homesteader.

Evening had begun to settle down before Jim realized that his cow was nowhere in sight: Usually she had grazed her fill and then lay down contentedly somewhere near at hand but this time she seemed to be gone. Without knowing of a cow's instinct to return to her home range before delivering her calf, Jim set out to look for tracks; these weren't too hard to find, as there had been spring rains that left the gumbo at a consistency which caused it to stick to the feet in big lumps or glide greasily underfoot on the sidehills. As darkness came on, snow began to fall and then increase as the wind shifted around to the north. Stumbling with weariness, half-running, crying and cursing in frustration he finally found the cow and got her home. By this time there was real storm, no shelter except the house and the cow was obviously going to have her calf.

Jim tied the cow to the foot of his bed, gave her home feed and bedding on the dirt floor, perched his few chickens on the foot rail facing a safe direction, stoked up the fire in the stove and fell into bed too tired to think of trying to eat or anything else but rest.

This must have been the storm of May 10, 1908 which killed so many sheep and other stock and it changed Jim from a boy to a man who ever afterward faced poverty, hardship, or any other adversity with a calm optimism.

There was a new calf in the morning, the storm was over, and after breakfast Jim set down in his new home to write to his wife.

His letter was mainly about the progress on the house, about how he planned to make a floor of flagstones (which they used for years afterward) and how they could all be together in early June. He would have a kitchen added on by then, with a dugout pantry and root-cellar extending back into the hill. They would have a coop for their chickens and fix some kind of barn for the cow, and maybe he could get some kind of job to get money enough for a horse or two. The description of his first night in that new home was made to sound like just a humorous incident. Well, maybe it was at that, compared to some of the rest of their homesteading days.

The family did arrive in June: The train got in about three in the morning and they spent the rest of the time until daylight in the lobby of the little hotel. No money was available for a room where the children could rest or wash up. The promised flagstone floor was laid and the lean-to kitchen was built but water had to be carried from the few pot-holes of run-off which remained after a rain or hauled all the way from the creek a mile away. Jim had managed to exchange work in his 'spare time' for a horse. A fifteen dollar horse when horses were bringing a good price if one had the money to pay for them. A big shambling black animal with a bony lump on one knee, he managed to live far longer than his former owner had anticipated and served the purpose of a horse for a couple of years.

Ground had to be broken for a garden and for a little patch of corn on the few level acres of their claim. A smaller garden patch was planted on a fairly level patch of gumbo near the house and that first summer there was enough rain to produce quite a good crop of vegetables. The first two or three years of newly broken ground allowed production of cantaloupes, muskmelon and watermelon, but the coyotes enjoyed a bit of fresh fruit for a change of diet as well as anybody and got away with a share of the crop.

Breaking could be done with the single horse hitched to the plow and allowed frequent rest but later in the summer when the corn needed cultivating another problem came up. They borrowed a cultivator but it was a two-horse outfit. The horse could pull it but something was needed to hold up the neck yoke on the other side of the tongue. Jim walked along holding up the neck yoke opposite the old horse while Lorna drove the 'team.' They probably could have hoed the corn by hand with less fuss and trouble but they were farming and hard work made up for inexperience.

DIGGING A WELL

Next came the problem of a well. After a couple of dry holes it was decided to dig in the very bottom of the coulee in hope of at least getting water for stock even if drainage did flow into the well at times. At about twelve feet the hole bottomed out in a solid sheet of rock; this seemed like the last straw added to the long list of discouragement and they both admitted later that they had silently prayed for help. During the night, Lorna dreamed that they had somehow drilled through the rock and found water and in the morning persuaded Jim to make one last try in the well. After chiseling and hammering through about a foot of sandstone, the drill went through and there was water, good, clean, drinkable, actual water and enough of it to serve all their needs. True, during a spring thaw or the occasional run-off from a heavy rain, surface water did at times run into the well but they built up some embankment to keep most surface drainage away.

Who of us could be too fussy about a well, anyway? Nobody could build a well platform or cover tight enough to keep out the determined rodent or snake that was desperate for a drink during dry times. There were occasions when our wells got to be where they didn't taste so good, but then a lot of the water didn't taste very good anyway and we sort of disregarded the difference for a while; finally there came a day when there was no doubt about it. The well needed cleaning; this meant rigging either a ladder or the windlass which had been used for digging the well in the first place and somebody went down with shovel, bucket on a rope and a small can or two for bailing. There might be a live water snake or two which had been able to survive by swimming, or a frog or two, but the gopher who had burrowed under the platform in search of water and the mouse or two who had followed in his barrow weren't alive any more and hadn't been for some time. After the well had been bailed dry, and there was rarely one which couldn't be, the accumulated mud or other debris was bailed out, the well cover made tight again and we settled back to the familiar flavor of our own individual well. Alkali usually, along with maybe a little sulphur, sod or the various flavors produced by the mixed soils of that ancient ocean-bed land. It was water, precious, indispensable, rare, illusive water which nearly everyone had dug and sweated for and we had learned to treasure it.

When the settlers finally dried out or starved out or just gave up in plain disgust, most of them moved on farther west. It was noticeable in later years that they had all gone to where there was plenty of water. Trees and greenery of course were a big attraction but running water was what stopped them and many stopped in the first area where they found it.

By the time 1910 rolled around, Jim and Lorna were fairly well established, compared to those who were just coming in. I think there was another baby or two; I just can't remember. A new one seemed to arrive every year and I know that one or two got there without help of a doctor. I was too young to think of such matters as anything but uninteresting routine that didn't affect me in any way.

When my Dad came to look for our claim in the Spring of 1910, Jim acted as locator and took him around the area. By that time all the desirable land within several miles of any town had already been filed on and, besides that, Dad had the idea of locating where there would be some open grazing land, available water, and fuel within a reasonable distance. He had some experience with that type of country and he had some small capital to work with.

On the day that they finally decided on a suitable location, the old horse that had been so lacking in spirit that no one expected him to exceed a shambling trot, decided to run away and head for home; he managed to smash one of the buggy wheels before he was caught and in order to have it repaired without making an extra ten mile trip, Dad carried it all the way home. Before they reached Jim's place they saw a prairie fire smoke several miles behind them but it had nearly caught up with them before they got home. Prairie fires there weren't dangerous as the ones in higher grass such as Minnesota and Dakota, produced in early days, and one could step over or through the blaze to burned off ground, but still they travelled rapidly and of course swept away whatever grazing there had been. Some of them seemed to start up with no apparent explanation. People experimented with broken glass or whatever else they could think of to find the cause. The nearest guess seemed to be that someone had dropped a match and then some mouse gnawed on it but no one came up with a definite answer.

Jim's mother and a younger brother and sister had come to live with them, and an older brother, with his wife, had taken up a claim several miles west of them. Conditions must have been pretty crowded at Jim's place but I cannot remember hearing complaint of inconvenience or hardship. The summer after we arrived, the younger brother contracted typhoid fever from drinking water at one of the town wells and nearly died, but he was cared for there in that little family room as a matter of course and life went on as usual.

HOMESTEADING

We saw very little of them until our first Christmas which I have described. Everyone was just too busy trying to make ends meet and to do whatever building they had planned. Winter roads, or lack of them, prevented any travel that wasn't necessary.

Jim had already established a routine of going away to Dakota for two or three months at a time on plumbing contracts in order to support the family. He would return with his proceeds of the job and pay bills as well as he could. There would be several evenings of shopping in the catalog for desperately needed clothing and shoes. Most of the time the kids went barefoot although dried gumbo and cactus doesn't make for pleasant walking.

For a week or two he would work frantically to haul wood and coal, do whatever improvement they could manage and haul stones for a flagstone porch or platform in front of the house. I'll wager that the stones are still in place although all other signs of the place must be gone long ago.

Rowland, the oldest son, nine months younger than I, had to grow up as man of the family, chopping wood, carrying water, fixing whatever broke down and helping to care for the younger ones. He never got to know what childhood was and still managed to have fun and retain an ambition and optimism which carried him on to several million dollars later in life.

I remember the family laughing about Rowland's first day of school: At that time, parents didn't usually take their kids to school the first day, introduce them to the teacher, get them signed up and go through the routine of starting school which we have now. We went to school, maybe had a fight or two while getting started to get acquainted with the other strangers and shambled into the schoolroom when the bell rang, simply because some of the more experienced kids led the way.

School usually started by the teacher sort of assigning seats as she thought might be the best arrangement and then called us to order, told us her name, wrote it on the blackboard for us and began asking the names of the pupils and writing them down. When Rowland's turn came to give his name he said simply Rowland. After several attempts to get his last name, the teacher finally asked "Well, what does your mother call you beside Rowland?" "Rowland, get wood," was his reply; that pretty much typifies his early childhood, as there always seemed to be some chore for him, but he always seemed to maintain a cheerful outlook and see the funny side of life.

By the time there were three of the family going to school, Jim had gotten a gentle black mare they had christened Black Beauty; Lorna would load all three kids on the horse and they would plod off to school. On arriving, the teacher would help them dismount, the horse would go home and the kids would walk home in the afternoon.

The horse got its name from the story by that title, of course, but it brings up the point that every evening at home no matter how frustrating the day had been, Lorna gathered her brood for a period of reading, a game of some sort, or some singing around their out-of-tune old piano.

A QUART OF SAPPHIRES

We awakened one morning on the farm to find Mother extremely worried and sure that something was terribly wrong at the Morrow household. Now a trip to town in the middle of the week was an unheard of thing unless there was some dire emergency but she insisted that they should go.

They found that the three oldest children had been stricken with spinal meningitis. Rowland was only slightly affected and survived with only a tendency toward rheumatism in his knees, but the other two, Russell and Luard, were left handicapped for life, Russell with a paralyzed right arm and Luard with defective legs which years later led to his death in a car accident.

There didn't seem to be any known treatment for meningitis but as the two boys showed some signs of recovery our doctor, a Doctor Morrison, located a machine for giving electric shocks that we all hoped would help rejuvenate the damaged nerves and muscles. Some doctor in Europe a few years before had come up with the idea that electric shock would cure a host of ailments and he had had a large following in his belief. The rig itself consisted of a marble slab about eighteen inches square with a rheostat and an alternating current generator turned by a crank. There were two cords terminating in metal grips. Take a grip in each hand, have someone turn the crank and you got a series of alternating electric shocks. The faster the crank was turned and the higher the rheostat was set, the more shock you got. Some of us amused ourselves by holding hands while someone cranked and trying to see how much current we could take. The treatment did no good, of course, but Dr. Morrison deserves tribute as another of the pioneer doctors who gave unstintedly of his time, skill and often his very limited finance to any and all who needed him. I rather suspicion, now, that it was he who paid for the machine.

A QUART OF SAPPHIRES

Who took me from my nice warm cot
Who set me on the cold, cold pot
Who made me whether I would or not?
My Mother.

So goes part of an old poem written long before my time and whoever, as a child, was wakened for this little ceremony in the middle of the night at twenty below zero in one of the old claim shacks has pushed that memory of pioneering way back in memory.

We hadn't heard anything about the psychological aspects of bed-wetting, but mothers who did the laundry in those times seemed to be light sleepers.

By the time the fourth child, a little girl, had arrived, the traditional china vessel was long gone and that universal container, the ten pound lard bucket, was in use. One winter morning before waking her little daughter, Lorna set this bucket to warm beside the heater; by the time she got the child up, one side of the vessel was not only warm, it was smoking hot! For some time there was a half ring branded on the little behind.

This daughter visited me recently: A frail little old lady now and I didn't ask her whether she still bore the lard bucket brand. Instead we reminisced about the fun and the little adventures of childhood that made claim-shack days seem pleasant.

We used to hunt agates along the railroad track as they were quite common in the gravel used for track ballast. Once in a while we would find a sapphire. She mentioned finding a large lemon yellow sapphire in the yard in front of their house and that she had sold it to one of the depot agents for two dollars.

The memory came back to me then that the man had had the stone cut into three settings. A ring for himself, his daughter and his son. He gave out the information that he had found it in his pigpen while watching the hogs eat. I can't think of a more unlikely place to find sapphires than the land where their place was but she said that her brother Rowland had told her shortly before he died that he had buried a quart jar full of them on the place when they were kids. He had evidently kept his findings a secret from the rest of us when he found better hunting than the railroad track.

There is no sign of the place now other than the stone floor and porch, but somewhere near there is a quart of sapphires.

BOOTLEGGING

When prohibition came, there was sort of a gradual change in the attitude of the people. There was the general feeling that the law had been sneaked into effect without the consent of the majority of voters and then, too, young men were coming home from the service who were already fed up with regulations and restrictions.

One of the very first to realize the possibility of profit was a farmer near Miles City. He was a well-established farmer, never drank and was altogether the staid, solid citizen. He either had previous experience at some distillery or got busy and learned how to produce fairly good liquor long before the average moonshiner even began to think about it. If anyone had noticed the smell of fermenting grain about the place they would have assumed that it was feed for the hogs. When the man had produced several barrels of liquor, he disposed of his still, sat back to age his product and shortly before time for the Miles City rodeo he went around to the various pool-halls for a visit with the proprietors. The small supply of bonded liquor that had been hoarded away was about gone and bootlegging mainly consisted of rum-running from Canada by car or the occasional airplane. Mr. Farmer took his orders in barrel lots, drove into town with his truckload one day and made his deliveries as matter-of-factly as though delivering a side of beef, deposited his receipts in the bank and went home. He was through with the bootlegging business before anybody else got started.

Before very long, half the ne'er-do-wells in the area were setting up stills and some of them turned out some pretty wicked stuff. The county authorities couldn't cope with the situation and furthermore didn't feel much like arresting some neighbor for an offense nobody believed in anyway.

Now about the time I got into high school there was a time when coyote hides brought a fairly good price, about ten dollars. A number of people got some coyote hounds, fixed a cage for them on the bank of their Model T Ford and set about catching coyotes. They would have a trap door to the cage that could be opened by jerking a rope from the driver's seat.

The coyotes promptly learned to run as soon as they saw one of these outfits, so the thing to do was to charge as near as possible with the truck, bounding over whatever the prairie offered in the way of rocks and sagebrush and then jerk open the trap-door. The hounds would roll end over end as they bounded out, look around for the fleeing coyote and the race was on. Quite a bit of excitement, and it wasn't long until one of the bootleggers got himself a pack of hounds. Here was a good excuse for a lot of driving around entailed by deliveries and of course a chance to stop in for a visit with any other still operator.

My high-school batching partner and I would sometimes go to the poolhall in the evenings and we would see the hunters come in at times to play pool and visit with friends.

The bootlegger-coyote hunting team was soon joined by a fellow who seemed to be quite an addition to the party. He was a beefy, red faced blowhard, full of stories and loud talk, buying drinks and being the life of the party. About ten days after Mr. Blowhard left, every bootlegger and still operator in the whole area was hauled into court. This boon companion turned out to be a federal agent. Probably on his next assignment he would portray the part of a preacher or banker with equal facility.

For the returning veterans, there was a vocational training program and one fellow took up dentistry. As I recall, the schooling must not have been anything like the training required now because he wasn't gone very long before setting up practice. Whatever, he finally became quite a competent dentist. He established his office in Ismay about the same time that pulling teeth was recommended for almost any ailment.

During an evening at the bar with a couple of friends, one of the fellows complained of rheumatism so immediately the doctor recommended having his teeth pulled. The topic was carried on through the evening along with the drinks so that by closing time, "C'mon up to the office, we'll fix that rheumatism right now. While we're at it you both might as well have it done and no more

LOST KANGAROO

of these aches and pains." When the boys woke up about noon the next day they hardly knew themselves. One was pretty upset about it and wished he'd kept his rheumatism but the other took it as one of the little jokes that life hands out at times.

LOST KANGAROO

The lost kangaroo episode must have happened some time during our homesteading days although we heard nothing of it until several years later, when the story was told to me by a Mr. Miller, who had spent sixteen years as advance man and purchasing agent for Ringling Brothers circus.

The show had arrived at Glendive when a small tornado struck them, damaging the tent and upsetting some of the wagons. During the storm, a kangaroo escaped.

The publicity man decided that here was a good news item and a way of advertising the circus, so he offered a reward of $100 for the lost animal without the least thought of ever seeing the beast again.

When the circus got to Miles City, an old rancher with four strapping big sons appeared, demanding the reward. One of the boys had roped the kangaroo and they had it tied down securely in a lumber wagon. Now here was something the publicity man hadn't foreseen. A hundred dollars was a lot of money in those days and the animal was safely back on the circus grounds so he set about claiming it with little or no payment. The ranchers were not about to be cheated and a fight started. The old circus rallying cry of Hey Rube went up and all the roustabouts swarmed in to help. The old man and his four boys got their backs together and whipped the whole circus crew to a standstill. In the melee the poor kangaroo was trampled to death. After the fight the rancher served an injunction against the circus, preventing them from leaving town until the hundred dollar reward was paid in full.

THE TOWN'S DEMISE

We didn't realize it at the time, but our community of first-comers who believed in a rosy future had already started to fall apart at the seams.

A couple by the name of Ellsworth had built the combined hotel, poolhall and store and later built their home on the edge of town on the shore of Fallon Creek. There were cottonwood trees for shade and I think by that time the railroad had drilled an artesian well for their own water supply and allowed the townspeople to put in mains.

The Ellsworth house was a large two-story building set high on a basement whose walls extended high enough for windows along the south side to make a pleasant, sunny room.

There was a full basement, divided down the middle by a partition and the stairs to the upper floor. The north half comprised of furnace space, coal bin, laundry and room for a shop and workbench. The south half held the kitchen and a long dining table. So far as I know, the Ellsworths had no children and it seemed as though some kind providence had planned and built the place for the Morrows.

THE TOWN'S DEMISE

Good fortune seemed to smile for a while. Jim had completed some profitable plumbing contracts and they were able to buy the house. They had some cows, a team and some chickens, there was plenty of good water, even enough, glory be, to water a garden. Wood was handy and plentiful and the kids could get to school with only a half mile walk.

Several years passed here. More children were born, one baby was found dead in bed one morning in the sudden way babies die at times. It was apparently all right except for a cold at six in the morning and was gone at eight. Another fell in a cistern which had been left open during cleaning and drowned. So it went, as in many other families: Good fortune, tragedy, progress, all mixed together.

As the town progressed, a church was built, clubs were formed and the high school got going. Lorna was active in all community activities, read to her kids at night, managed to help and care for any neighbor and no matter how scant the groceries, there was always room for the kids who flocked to visit them.

I sometimes think the whole family must have blocked out some of the hardship and tragedy simply by determining to face each day as it came and make the best of it. Jim's father had been a vaudeville stage jigger at one time and Jim had taught himself to jig just by watching him. I remember hearing the happy rhythms of his feet one evening as he jigged to some tune on the phonograph. He was upstairs in the living room alone while we were all in the basement kitchen at some game. He was just serene and happy to be at home and at peace for a few days between the jobs when he had to be away.

HOMESTEADING

As the Model T Ford took over from the horse and buggy, and the town began to die, the livery barn came up for sale cheap. It was a lot of building; big, with, of course, a loft for hay above the lower floor. Lorna bought it. The Morrows had always raised cows and poultry, so here was a building they could make good use of. I don't know how they got the thing moved, but after getting it in place, Lorna and the kids set about building a high stone foundation under it and did a fine job of it.

We didn't realize at the time that our town had started to decline. This was about the first business to close but as time went on, people moved away and others failed to take their places, the lumber yard burned down, a tornado took the town hall, leaving the piano sitting forlornly in its place with the sheet music still on the rack. Houses were moved away to other locations and little by little the town just withered away like some plant that dries and loses its leaves so slowly that the owner continues to hope for survival.

The railroad had furnished some support for the town as there had been busy train traffic and the trains stopped there for water and coal, the train crews ate at the restaurant and quite a lot of cattle and grain were shipped out, but when the diesel locomotives came into use, so did the dry years and the depression curtail shipping. The coal docks, which had elevated the coal for the locomotives was blasted down, the water tank sold and the depot and section houses disposed of.

The Morrows, the Clarks and a few others who had helped to build the town were the last of those first settlers to leave. They hung on until some time in the depression and a few people came to take their places, but an era had passed.